All the Days

Walking with God Through Friendship,
Singleness, and Summer Camp

Abby Friend

DEDICATION

To the women who have walked this life alongside me, pushing me towards God with their faithfulness

CONTENTS

PROLOGUE

This isn't the story I wanted to tell.

I've thought about writing a book for a long time. Someday, I thought. I didn't know when someday would come or exactly what I'd say when it did, but I figured it would be something along the lines of how I followed God through my life, doing what He'd asked me to do, and how I got all I wanted because of it. I would tell about traveling and living the single life and working at a summer camp. I wanted the moral of the story to be, "I didn't date much or party hard, but God led me into a great marriage with 2.5 children, lots of friends, an amazing community and a job I love. I was faithful to God, and he was faithful to me."

The more I thought about it, though, the more I realized that the someday I had in my mind was the day all the hard things of life were behind me. My dreams had come true and my hopes had come to fruition. I hadn't arrived, per se, but pretty much. When I pinpointed this thought, I was able to bring myself into the reality that the someday of my subconscious does not exist. Sure, I haven't dated much and certainly have not partied hard, and I've tried to be faithful to God, but the hard things of life continue to spring up. However, the hard is mixed in with a whole lot of good, and what I've realized is all of that speaks of God's faithfulness. The fact that God is in the good and in the hard is the reality of life, and that's the story that needed to be told.

I started thinking about the conversations I'd had with my friends, who are wonderful and normal, not fatally flawed or weird (as if that's the hold up), but are still yearning for something – a husband or a family or the perfect job or some guidance or direction. When I spoke to friends who were recently divorced or still waiting for that guy to realize how great they are or still waiting to have babies or land that dream job, I heard echoes of what God wants for all of us - community, families, relationships, fulfillment. In these conversations there's always talk of adventures and world travels, new business ideas and making the world a better place, but also often a little wounded-ness and heartache woven in amidst the laughter and the joy. Because that is where life happens, in the tension between the two, never having totally arrived in pure bliss, but not allowing disappointments and struggles of life to totally derail all that is good. Everyone wants to live a full, meaningful life, but how do you do that when things don't turn out quite like you hoped and the longing feels more prevalent than anything else?

For me, the longing revolves around wanting a family of my own, a husband and kids (more than 2.5 of them). When I looked around I realized hardly anyone over the age of 25 is talking about living the single life; they are also still desiring marriage and a family, but wondering if it will come or if we missed it altogether. There aren't many conversations about how fun it is to have the freedom to come and go as you please and travel the world, but still want to be tied down too. Very few people ask the questions out loud that are asked within your inner circle, not pointedly mind you, but cloaked in sighs and unfinished sentences – if God has answered so many of my prayers, why hasn't he answered this one, the one I want the most? And is it even worth it to wait for God to work in my circumstances when I could just do things my own way? What if He doesn't come through this time?

Many of the people I know answered these questions themselves, rather than waiting on God, and the conclusion many of them came to is that it's not worth it to trust Him. And not unlike Adam and Eve in the garden, their decisions and sometimes their mouths said, "God didn't come through for me when I thought He would. I'm hurt or lonely or bored or insecure, and God didn't really mean what He said about all these things. He cannot be trusted to give me what's best." They walked away from God or from his best for them.

"Wait!" I wanted to shout. "You're not alone! You're not the only one waiting or the only one disappointed." It can be so hard to trust God, to walk with him through all of our days – the lonely, fantastic, exciting and boring days. The days of dreams coming true and the days of disappointment that will take you out at the knees. The days of traveling foreign lands and the days spent sitting in an office. The days when you think you'll never be okay again and the days you wish would never end. But those are the days that make up all of life, the ups and the downs and the ins and the outs of each moment of triumph and defeat.

So, no, this is not the story I wanted to write, but I think it's a richer story than the story of someday. It is not the story of how every aspect of my life came together perfectly. But it is the stories of my life that tell of God's faithfulness in the waiting, in the singleness and disappointments, in the friendships and the fun, and of so many days spent at summer camp.

ABROAD

Torres, not *torros*. Towers, not bulls. As I lay in bed only a few days after I'd arrived in Spain, I realized my blunder. My host family had been talking to me about the anniversary of September 11th, not the running of the bulls. I had pretended to understand, but I'm sure my fake smile and sheepish nodding gave me away. I wanted to understand, and maybe more importantly for them to think I understood, but everything was out of context for me. I was studying abroad, just like I had wanted, but this wasn't the time of my life I thought it would be.

I had grand expectations of studying abroad in Europe. I envisioned walking cobblestone streets to picturesque views of mountains or cityscapes. I thought every day would have something new to discover – winding streets full of history, old houses and buildings each telling me a story I couldn't wait to hear. I imagined becoming the best of friends with my fellow students, getting lost in foreign towns together, laughing long into the night, meeting strangers with castles or Vespas who would take us on adventures only locals knew about (this was clearly before I'd seen the movie *Taken*). I thought my host family would become a second family, people I would keep in touch with forever, sending Christmas cards and visiting again when I had my own family. I thought I would find myself like Sabrina did – coming back to the States hardly recognizable to those who knew me best – with a new confidence, a broader world view, fluent in another language, with a richer and fuller life, now a better version of myself. Or maybe I would meet the love of my life, a Spaniard or an American also studying abroad, and we'd craft a great love story set to the backdrop of little cafes and walks on romantic, far away shores. I thought it would be easy – so full of new experiences and life that I wouldn't miss home at all. And sure I'd go to class, but that was secondary to weekend trips and immersing in the culture.

While I packed my bags for a semester in Santander, a coastal town in northern Spain, I had my sister's voice echoing in my head. "You'll get a true cultural experience by going somewhere they don't speak English. If you go to an English speaking country, you might as well stay in America." I grew more and more nervous as my departure date came closer. I still wanted to go, of course, but my confidence was shaking as I prepared to actually live with a family in a foreign country for three months. I cried in the airport as I hugged my mom goodbye, surprising myself and wishing I could hold in the tears. I was a brave 19 year old. I had wanted this. This would be fine. I would be fine.

After an all-night flight to Madrid and a five-hour bus ride north to Santander, my nervousness began to subside a little. My fellow students were all nice enough, although they seemed so much more sure of themselves than I was feeling. But man, that bus ride was beautiful. We drove through the

Spanish countryside and stopped for lunch at a quintessential European town. The village rose in the distance, a beacon of quaintness just waiting to be explored. There were cobblestone streets and a spire of some kind – a former monastery, I found out. I couldn't believe I was finally in Spain. And maybe because of my sleepy state, it felt dreamlike. I was really doing this. I was actually going to spend a semester living in Europe, just like I had wished and planned. This cute little town offered me some hope. Maybe things would be every bit of the adventure I was longing for.

The bus finally arrived in Santander at dusk. It pulled up to a small group of people looking expectant, waiting for their foreign exchange students. I watched my fellow students meet their host families, uncomfortably greeting them and swiftly loading into waiting cars or taxis. My host mother, who soon became known as "madre", was late, and I had that panicky feeling you get when your mom is running late to pick you up from school. Was she coming? Did she forget? Will I be left standing alone here in the dark? But, of course, just like my mom always arrived at school, my host mom did come.

She was small -- a head and shoulders shorter than me with short dark wavy hair and pleasantly plump. And she wore lipstick. I was greeted with a kiss on each cheek, and we took a taxi back to the apartment I would share with her and her daughter for the next three months. I had a panicky feeling then too. I had only known my fellow study abroad students since the night before, and we'd only traveled and slept since we'd met, but they were American and they spoke English. And then we were separated.

My madre and I arrived at the apartment building and took the elevator to the third floor. My new home. It smelled of cigarette smoke, but had the nice, comforting, outdated feeling of your grandmother's house. I settled my stuff in my room, tried to make some small talk with my madre and her daughter, and my new *familia* pointed me to a pay phone so I could call my family back in the States. I used my calling card to dial home and before my mom even answered, I was bawling. What was I doing here? How did I get here? Did I really want to do this? I am so tired! It dawned on me how far away I was from all things familiar. I had wanted to be brave, to strike out on my own, to do this thing by myself. But now, standing on this street corner, calling my family thousands of miles away, I was drowning in a sea of emotions as wide as the Atlantic I had just crossed – homesickness, fear, isolation, and now embarrassment that I was crying within minutes of arriving. This was not how I expected to feel on my first evening of my adventure. I tried to hide my face in the pay phone, imagining my new host family watching me lose it from their window, pity in their eyes, wondering what they'd signed themselves up for. After a quick update to my family that I had arrived safely and a tearful goodbye, I went back up to my apartment and tried unsuccessfully to convince my madre I was fine. My puffy eyes gave me away, and her concerned frown told me she didn't buy it.

No one told me that being brave can also feel scary, and that that thing I always wanted to do will not magically be awesome. It might, but maybe it will be awesome in ways other than what I was expecting.

By the next morning, after some sleep, I was feeling a little more at peace and adventurous. Our group took a bus tour and a boat tour of the bay over the next couple days. I got a feel for the lay of the land, and explored the town on foot, a bit cautiously, but with excitement for what this city held. I sat down on a bench by the bay, looking out over the calm, vibrant blue waters and mountains in the distance. "God, help me never to take this view for granted. Help me to relish in it every single time I see it," I prayed. "I don't want to grow accustomed to it, to lose the sense of wonder I feel right now."

It wasn't long before I discovered the best two things about Santander – the beaches and the ice cream. I went to the beach all the way into October before it got cold, and I loved the beach town vibe. It was so convenient to hop on a bus or take a walk and be relaxing on the beach in less than 30 minutes. After a couple afternoons at the beach, my madre told me that she could tell I'd been in the sun – I was no longer *blancisima* (really white). There were several beaches to choose from, and I wanted to try them all. It was a cultural experience each time. There were topless women everywhere. Moms, grandmas, didn't matter. The signs for "*no nudismo*" apparently didn't mean what I thought they meant. The grandmas had this ingenious invention, a large piece of fabric that fit over their head and tied around their neck. They would change clothes under that thing. Brilliant! And then there was the ice cream, the *helado*. It tasted so much better in Spain. I don't even know how. Creamier, maybe. Or sweeter. Something made it the best euro fifty I'd ever spent. And so I got ice cream almost every single day. I was obsessed. It was like it was calling out to me, telling me I needed it to bring me comfort, to bring me sweet pleasure. Even if everything else wasn't as I wanted it to be, the ice cream knew what I needed. But that *helado* betrayed me, doing its best to help me pack on a few pounds, and in the end bringing such finite satisfaction.

While it was warm, if I wasn't at the beach, I would spend some afternoons down on the Presidio, the area that stretched along the waterfront with shops, parks, and benches, perfect for people watching. Everyone was outside – moms pushing their strollers, older couples enjoying the view of the bay, kids running about. One afternoon, I took my journal to capture some of my thoughts, and sat on a bench amidst the flurry of activity. An older man sitting nearby struck up a conversation with me in Spanish. His gray hair peeked out from under his hat, and with a smile he told me of his granddaughter who could speak English. He said that before I left Spain, I would be fluent in Spanish. I smiled, believing him, wanting it to be true, even though I didn't really know how to tell him that.

There were moments, aside from the ice cream and *la playa*, when I really loved Spain – when we traveled especially. The feeling of exploring a new place and visiting places I'd studied about in my high school Spanish classes is what I had imagined every day would be like. There were castles and palaces, aqueducts and art museums. My fellow students and I traipsed down Las Ramblas in Barcelona, taking pictures with the living statues, laughing as they came alive when we gave them a few coins. We rappelled down waterfalls in Potes and stayed in a hostel we had booked for ourselves over the phone in Spanish! I tried new foods at roadside restaurants and practiced my Spanish in shops and on the street, asking for directions. I started to be able to communicate quite well, even though I often felt insecure about my skills and found speaking harder than understanding, but I could tell that I was improving. I bought souvenirs at small markets and only occasionally went to Starbucks in big cities for a taste of home. There was so much beauty to behold in Spain, in the old cities of Toledo and Sevilla and in the small towns in between. I spent several bus rides looking out the window at the farmland and the hills, amazed that people lived here – here in the lush green countryside with seemingly nothing else around for miles. What would my life be like if I lived here? I'd wonder from the comfortable bus seat. I'd think about where I'd shop and go to school and how it would be totally different to live on a farm in northern Spain than to go college in Raleigh, North Carolina.

But, as much as the cultural things were new and exciting, the everyday living in Santander was slow. We only took a couple hours of classes a day, so I had plenty of time to miss home. I really wanted to spend my time productively. I was living abroad! Where were the adventures? Where were the great locals? I would probably never do this again (in fact, this trip cemented in my mind that I didn't really want to live abroad for a long period of time again – good to know), so I felt that I should take full advantage of it. But I didn't know how. There were a lot of things I felt I should be doing. I should talk to my host family more. I should try to find a church to attend. I should explore every far-flung piece of the city. I should exercise. But I just didn't. Even though I did become friends with some fellow students, I spent a lot of time by myself. And when the weather got cold, I spent a lot of time indoors. I took full advantage of the siesta, taking a nap every single day. I wrote in my journal a lot, sometimes just about the happenings at home that I'd been emailed about. I listened to music. I spent a lot of time in the computer lab at school because there was unlimited

Internet access, which meant unlimited time to email, chat on instant messenger, or read about pop culture.

I longed for the excursions we took as a group because that meant I was out of the house and out of the routine. I counted down the days until I could go home. It wasn't that I was miserable. I was so thankful I had the opportunity to be there, living in an apartment on Menendez Pelayo, but I longed for something more, something else I didn't quite know how to describe or attain. The traveling was great, because I was on the go, exploring, seizing the day. But when it came to settling in, becoming part of a new family and a new city, I didn't know how to do that.

It wasn't like college, exactly, where there are built in friends everywhere you look. I didn't have a safety net or the sense of security that comes when you're home or near all things familiar. So much of life and therefore my friendships had come from Christian community. There was youth group in high school and Campus Crusade and Bible study in college. But there weren't many Christian churches around Santander, and even though I enjoyed the one I attended a few times in the beginning of the semester, it was difficult to get to and I eventually stopped going.

The church met in the bottom floor of what appeared to be an apartment building, although there were not many residents around, making it feel forgotten and old. The couple times I attended, I experienced peace and such warmth just by being in the dimly lit room cooled by ceiling fans with fellow believers who all smiled and said *hola*. There were several countries represented in the congregation, but we worshipped in Spanish with songs that I knew in English. I even understood most of the major points of the sermons that were also delivered in Spanish, of course. God met me there, in the way He does when people gather in His name. It was such a nice respite for my soul to be there. It was like getting a hug when you've been away from physical touch for a while. The church community felt so inviting and so familiar. And yet, after only a few times there, I stopped going. I should have tried. I should have forced myself to figure out the buses and to get up a little earlier, so that I could have the community that church offered.

The most community I experienced outside of my American classmates was with my host family. They were so gracious. My madre got up every morning and fixed me hot chocolate and unwrapped some cookies for me, even though I'm sure she'd have rather slept in, and I really could have made breakfast myself. I would sit in the kitchen before class, usually alone, staring out the window at the ivy-covered wall across the street, wondering if I was getting all that I could out of this experience. What should I try to say to my madre today? How can I make small talk with my *hermana*? I was always at a loss, and often just listened to their chatter or kept my thoughts to myself. My madre was quiet with me, but kind. We watched TV together sometimes, *Gran Hermano* or American shows dubbed in Spanish. One time she had friends over to play cards. I came home to the apartment filled with cigarette smoke and laughter. I sat in my room and listened as they laughed and sang and played cards. This is a moment I wanted to remember forever, I thought. And I wish I had had the gusto to ask to join them.

I don't like to regret, which I know is not unique to me, but I try to live life to the fullest in the moment so that I won't regret missing anything later. I like to think that I did the best I could at the time, and I try not to worry about it now. But looking back at my time in Santander, I wish I had engaged more. I wasn't snobby or too cool for school, which is maybe how I appeared - I was just insecure. I was nervous to look dumb or sound dumb or to not be understood. I smiled and was polite, but I just couldn't force myself to move beyond that.

The closer I got to my departure date, the happier I was. I started packing to go home a week before I left. It's not like I had that much stuff, I was just ready. And finally, on a chilly December morning, I trudged my stuff down to the bus waiting outside. My madre walked me out and got a little teary as we said goodbye, hugging me and kissing me on both cheeks. She said I'd been like a daughter to her. I was touched by her emotion, and as much as I wanted to return the sentiment, I just felt relief. I'd made it. I'd spent a whole semester in Spain, speaking a different language, making my way.

When I got home everyone asked me if I missed it. And the truthful answer was no. In fact, I wanted to call everyone I knew and people I didn't, just so I could speak in English ("Hello, AT&T. I just wanted to speak to someone on the phone in English. And also turn my cell phone back on.") I truly did enjoy my time there, I had no regrets about going, but I was ready to be back in the familiar. I may not have experienced a total transformation like Sabrina, but when I got back I held my head a little higher and walked a little taller. I wasn't quite so nervous about life - to strike out on my own, talk to that new person, and certainly not to travel by myself.

And being in Spain did help me discover myself, although maybe not quite in the ways I had hoped. I discovered I was insecure and sometimes lacked self-control, basically that I was imperfect. That's a tough thing to learn about yourself, especially when you want so badly to have it all together, to thrive in every situation, to be all you want to be. But sometimes it's enough just to go, just to be there, just to do the best you can. Show up, buy that plane ticket, set a goal and complete it, even if it's scary and hard. There's a lot to be said for that. It would look different if I lived abroad now, but I'm glad I did it then – when I was unsure about the unknown, but I went anyway.

ABBY FRIEND

MOUNTAINTOP SUMMERS

After working as a camp counselor in college, I would return to school after a beautiful summer in the Blue Ridge Mountains, sit in my dorm room and long to be back at camp. My heart actually ached to be there. I loved the people, the ministry, the kids, the games, all of it, and I wanted to be back in those majestic hills. I would listen to "Walk Down This Mountain" by Bebo Norman on repeat and resolve to keep my "heart held high". I can't even tell you what that song is about exactly, but the sentiment of leaving a mountain top and going back down to the real world was something I had experienced so deeply, and Bebo seemed to be the only one who understood.

I had wanted to be a camp counselor as long as I could remember, which was odd considering I'd never been to camp as a kid. My sister applied to be a camp counselor once. She didn't take the job due to a scheduling conflict, but I remember being 11 or 12 years old, examining the camp brochure she had, being wowed by the amount of fun everyone was having in those pictures. I wasn't interested in being a camper necessarily, just working at a camp when I got into college. In middle and high school, I'd spent a few weekends on retreats at camps, but that, along with several viewings of The Parent Trap and Salute Your Shorts, was the extent of my camp experience. So I really had very little idea what I was signing up for when I applied (and got the job!) for a camp counselor position at a camp in Asheville, North Carolina.

Arriving at camp was daunting at first, but it didn't take long for me to recognize that this was going to be a good job and a very fun summer. The camp property in and of itself was something special. Entering the gates was stepping into something sacred. It felt different, like holy ground. The sky seemed bluer, the clouds puffier and closer, like I could just reach up and touch their soft edges. The canopy of green trees kept the air cool and insulated from the heat of summer. To sit in a rocking chair on the dining hall porch overlooking the mountains and bask in the afternoon sun was to feel God's face shine upon you. I just knew God was there on that mountain top, and He seemed more real, more present, more available. It was clear God had been at work on that property for many years before I was there, and for several summer weeks I was able to step into a small piece of the story He'd been telling. Not only could I feel God there, I felt different there, more known and more me. Even though the days were busy and the hours were long, I was at peace and I felt like camp fit me just right. Camp was an easy place to let the weight of the world – the reality of my normal life at school with friend drama and weird family dynamics – melt away as I drove the winding, dirt road out to the heart of camp. That property set a beautiful stage for summer, but the fellow staff and campers played principal roles in what would become one of the most impactful seasons of my life.

The people, the fellow counselors and staff, although way funnier and cooler than me in my estimation, were my kind of people – laid back, lovers of the outdoors, fun-loving, and wanted to spend their summer doing something meaningful. They were an eclectic bunch filled with some of the kindest, funniest, most entertaining people I've ever met. There was an easy rapport among the staff, and everyone seemed free to be themselves, letting their quirky personalities shine. Something about camp just brings out everyone's truest self. People are free to laugh louder, be sillier, expose their hidden dancing/banjo-playing/belly-flopping talents. There's a level of comfort that camp entices out of people. Maybe it's being around kids constantly or running on little sleep, but everyone lets their guard down a bit and just is who they are. That was so refreshing after being in school where everyone feels the need to prove themselves and put on airs. In the summer, I could leave behind that pressure, not wear makeup and tell my corniest jokes, and that was the norm.

Of course, I still carried my insecurities with me. I was never quite sure if I was doing a good enough job or making a difference. I wasn't the most outgoing or the most carefree or the most athletic counselor, but I tried to remember that everyone brought something different to the table. John told us stories about childhood adventures with his brother, bringing them to life with vivid details, everyday things made hilarious because we were at camp and under his spell of being a standout counselor. I secretly wished I was a little more like Melody, a free spirit with absent-minded quirkiness, able to make everything fun, including oversleeping and coming in late to breakfast ("It's pajama day! Let's go!"). Blaine had an uncanny ability to impersonate a pterodactyl, which came in handy surprisingly often. Tara, one of my supervisors, made sure everyone knew she cared about them personally; she brought tea parties to my porch and "kidnapped" me in a van to hear about my week. And, even though I didn't have an obvious talent or an over the top personality, I tried to remember that I could connect with my campers in a way others could not. God uses quieter, steady camp counselors too, and it was okay to just be myself.

There were times in the throes of the summer when I'd stop and look around the dining hall at the other counselors interacting with their campers, and I'd be so thankful that I was on the team. I felt like I was a part of a very elite club where the only requirements were loving Jesus and kids and being a willing participant in what God was doing – and an occasional messy game, relay race or unclogging of a toilet. Being on camp staff was being in the best kind of mutual admiration society. And being around these counselors, I felt caught up into something bigger than myself, united with people excited to be there for one common goal – to tell kids about Jesus. And that's what brought us back summer after summer. It certainly wasn't for the money. Everyone worked for pennies per hour (we discouraged each other from doing the math on the paycheck, because it was dismal), so only the truly dedicated wanted the job and stuck it out.

As counselors we spent our whole day with the kids, save for an hour off each day. There was a lot of time to build a foundation for influence in our relationships with them. It was tough at times, depending on the age and personality of the kids in the cabin. After having a 10 year old girl who was obsessed with wolves, acting like one at times and asking us to call her by her dog name, Maxi, I realized working with older girls might be more in my strengths. I learned to love the middle school age – the girls were old enough to have meaningful conversations and ask heartfelt questions, but young enough to still buy in to skits and messy games. It was humbling and exciting to have the opportunity to teach these girls about the truths of who God is and how much He loves them. I was honored to be entrusted to lead them in Bible study every day, and I spent time praying about what I should teach them, preparing stories and activities. I loved taking my campers down to the old amphitheater for our Bible study time. It was off the beaten path, secluded, but convenient. Under those trees, on those old wooden benches, where campers had sat for many years before us, we talked about things like love, spending time in God's Word, prayer and trust. And after I taught them, I tried to exemplify those things in the way I lived my life. The beauty and the reality of camp is that the campers saw both the good and the bad in me, seeing me practice what I preached, but then also seeing tired and grumpy me (although hopefully not as much). I learned humility when, after teaching a lesson on loving others, I got more and more frustrated with my campers for not listening. A camper asked me, "Are we being hard to love?" I was caught, needing my own reminders, thankful my campers had been listening and called me out. The staff walked with the campers through life together for one week, modeling how we can be followers of Jesus, still live life fully and be fun people to top it off.

And boy, camp was fun! Monday afternoons were reserved for Pool Olympics. There were relay races and biggest splash competitions. There was wrestling among counselors on pool floats and the infamous belly flop contest, judged by how level the body was upon entrance into the pool, the sound of the stomach hitting the water and the redness of skin afterwards. My favorite was the creativity displayed in the "synchronized swimming" competitions complete with lifting campers in the air and dramatic fanning of arms and kicking of legs. And spirit points were always awarded for the team with the most creative cheers (a favorite became, "Fill it! Plug it! Constipate that bucket!" for a game of plugging a leaking barrel while trying to fill it to overflowing). Pool Olympics was simple, yet it embodied the joy of camp for me. It was outside, kids being kids, a healthy dose of encouragement from counselors and fellow campers, and enthusiasm abounded.

While camp was certainly fun, there were parts that could be stressful too – namely the campout. Every cabin went on a campout each week, rain or shine. There was a lot of pressure associated with the campout, because there was the potential for so many memorable moments and life lessons. A lot of times the walls campers had put up the whole week came crumbling down in the darkness around the campfire, since they were even more out of their element and had built solid relationships with their fellow campers and counselors by that point in the week. But before that could happen, it was up to the two counselors in each cabin to set up camp, build the campfire, cook food over said fire, and keep everyone entertained, safe and sane without losing our cool. Not a small task, especially when dealing with 12 thirteen year old girls. Even if it wasn't currently raining, it always seemed to have just recently rained which made fire building, as well as staying dry (one of the cardinal rules), very tricky. Keeping the girls entertained was another challenge, not to mention hoping for life change to happen too. There were many times the campers were stuck in the tent playing games while my assistant counselor and I got soaked in a downpour, keeping the fire going and heating up corn and hot dogs. If there were great, God moments happening in the tent, we were not privy to them.

Occasionally though, it was dry and cool, and everything aligned for a perfect campout. It was a well-earned bragging right, wet weather or not, if you could get a blazing fire going with just one match. One night, after a few rough campouts under my belt, I did it. That campout turned out to be one of the best. Fire building was normally such a stressor, and I can't tell you how many fires I prayed over (actually, I can – all of them), but when I got that fire going and those girls fed under the canopy of trees in the lush forest, that was a camp dream. We sat around on fallen logs as makeshift benches, laughing and telling stories until the fireflies came out and lit up the night. We were dry, we were well fed, and everyone was happy. I thanked God over and over that evening for being so faithful, for caring about the smallest details including my one-match fire.

On Thursdays, after camping out, the older campers would hike the infamous Rappel Trail. It was a few miles through the woods and a lot of uphill to the cliff where we would rappel, hence the name. There was lots of talk among the staff of whose cabin hiked it fastest, whose cabin ran down after rappelling, who was running late because they had to push their campers, sometimes literally, up those inclines. I mostly stayed quiet about the whole thing, even though my stomach would be in knots for days leading up to it. I was not a big fan of the Rappel Trail. I think it was equally a mental obstacle for me as well as a physical one.

Before camp I hadn't ever really hiked, and I wasn't used to pushing myself physically. The one real mountain hike I had done was on the first day I reported to work at camp after I'd been there for staff training and had gone home for the first half of the summer. I got there on a day between camp sessions and some fellow counselors were headed to nearby waterfalls for hiking and rock hopping. I thought it sounded fun, but having never done anything like that before I didn't know to bring water or that having eaten beforehand would be a major key to my success. My legs started shaking on the way to the waterfall, which was all downhill. I tried not to think about the return trip. The day was great, really fun bonding with the fellow staff, but when it came time to return to our cars, I was sluggish going back uphill, worn out, not having food or water in my system and not having been active during my five weeks at home (ahem, out of shape). My only saving grace was that a fellow counselor had fallen on a rock and hurt her knee, and she required major assistance on the way back up which slowed everyone down considerably. I hated to be thankful for her injury, but I was at that moment. Otherwise, I surely would have been left behind, adding to my embarrassment that I couldn't keep up and letting everyone know I was not cut out to be an outdoorsy camp counselor.

That one hiking memory stuck in my psyche, and every week the thought of the Rappel Trail brought back feelings of being ill equipped and slow, and somehow I knew I would be exposed as a faker because I didn't love every minute of losing my breath. But, hike the Rappel Trail I must. So each Thursday morning after a Pop Tart breakfast, I gathered my girls at the start of the trail, told them how this was going to be hard but not impossible, and that we weren't going to

24

complain. We prayed together, I took a deep breath, and we started our hike. The pep talk was mostly for me, but I'd like to think it helped the campers too. God was so real to me on those hikes, as cheesy as it may sound, because I didn't think I had the physical strength to go up one more time, and often the campers didn't either, but we struggled together and overcame. Every week my cabins made it up and down that trail safely and without any real incident. A hiker I became, even for just a few hours, but with great moments of euphoria after each successful trip.

I've heard it said that being a camp counselor is the hardest job you'll ever love, and that was certainly true for me. I didn't just need God for the obvious physically challenging things. There were times I didn't have the strength to get up and shower each day, especially as the summer wore on. Every day was a process in learning to die to myself, to lean on God's strength, to trust that He was with me. When my alarm went off in the morning (too early, in my estimation), I would pray for strength to get up and do it all over again. Wake the campers, encourage them to read their Bibles, serve them at breakfast, lunch, and dinner, teach them how to put up a tent or play a new game, dress up for Counselor Hunt and hide in a place where it was not too difficult to be found. Each day I was reminded of my need for God. There were days that required patience I didn't have – like when the toilet overflowed in our cabin twice in the same day, and I spent our rest time mopping the floor instead of napping. I learned to lean on God for energy because after six weeks of camp my introverted self could not get recharged in just one hour off a day. And, even though there weren't many things about camp I didn't like, there were still times I had to muster enthusiasm from the depths of me for one more round of floor polo. I wanted to serve, love, and play with my campers, because that is what I signed up for, and that is what Jesus would do, but that was a choice I had to make every single morning and sometimes multiple times throughout the day. I did survive each day, and dare I say I even thrived some days, because God was faithful to come through with all that I needed and more each day and each week of camp.

Because of the lessons I was learning and the ways I was growing spiritually, working at camp was so much more than a summer job. It was a holy experience for me. It was a beautiful thing to get away to the safety of the mountains, walk with Jesus and his people, and learn from Him so I could pour out to others. Sure, as a counselor I was stretched to the limits of myself, and I came to understand how finite my energy, patience and love really are. But in that, I also found the joy of walking closely with God, leaning on Him for all I needed. He met me in worship, in conversation, in laughter, and in community. And as the summer wound to a close, even though I was physically sapped of my energy, my spirit felt stronger and better equipped, ready to go back to my regular life. I truly was able to leave camp with "my heart held high". Bebo would have been proud.

TOPPING IT OFF

I went in to my third summer at camp knowing it would probably be my last. I was going into my senior year of college, and I knew what that meant – the real world was waiting. Over the past two years I had fallen in love with camp, so much so I thought I might pursue working in camping full-time after graduation. The year round staff at my camp was small, so I didn't even think I would have a chance to get a job there, but surely there were other camp jobs that would be equally as appealing. Therefore this summer was to be a glorious capstone of such a rich and impactful season in a place where I'd grown so much. But I just wasn't ready to let camp, specifically this camp, out of my grip. I prayed fervently all summer that God would provide closure in my heart about moving on. I needed it, because otherwise the sadness would be too much.

Leading up to that summer I read John Eldredge's book *Waking the Dead*. In it he talks about doing what makes your heart come alive, and as I read I got so excited because it confirmed what I thought was true – God wanted a good life for me and in this stage of my life that meant a job I could be passionate about. I spent so much time in college answering questions about what I would do after graduation. I was majoring in Communications, with a concentration in Interpersonal Communication, but I had no idea what I would do with that. It was interesting to me, which is why I picked it, and I didn't see any reason why I should spend four years studying something I didn't like. People would always ask, "What are you going to do with that degree?" as if it had never occurred to me that college was supposed to prepare me for a career. But the longer I worked at camp, the more I felt that is what I wanted to do. Camp fit me. It made my heart come alive. A camp job seemed improbable, maybe even far-fetched, but I wanted to go for it, and so I boldly started answering with that – "I want to work at camp full time."

I spent that third summer as a member of the Senior Staff, playing a support role with 15 or so other older college students, rather than being a counselor. Being on that small team, I felt like I had arrived to the inner circle of leadership and friendship. There were privileges and perks to being on Senior Staff, not the least of which was more free time in the day. However, it was during this time I realized how much I like structure and being busy. I never felt like I was doing enough. Were the directors pleased with my performance? Shouldn't I be doing more with my days? Everyone else seemed busier than me, which made me feel insecure, like I wasn't pulling my weight. Nobody wants to be the weak link, especially at camp, and I felt the need to prove that I was a worthwhile member of the staff. This pressure was self-imposed, and I learned later, a common misconception among staff that the directors were watching every move, just waiting for us to screw up. In fact, the directors were far too busy for that and were generally pleased with the staff, and while the desire to work hard was a good one, I also just had to learn to do my best with what I'd been given to do.

Therefore, because my job specifically had more free time, I used it to write everyone on staff an encouragement note – not necessarily productive, but it's always nice to be on the receiving end of a kind note. I took naps occasionally. And I spent time with my friends, helping them do their jobs when I could. I ran errands with Jen, who I met at camp the year before and who became a good friend that school year back at our university. I helped Rachel and Adam fold tarps after campouts. I also supervised the younger kitchen staff on Tuesdays, Aaron's day off. Part of my actual job was to help Emily and Andrew with games and skits, which I felt was my sweet spot. Being able to help in these areas made me realize I really enjoyed playing a support role, doing a lot of behind the scenes tasks. It takes a lot of people and positions to run summer camp, and I loved getting a small taste of so many of them.

The Tuesdays I spent in the kitchen were enjoyable because of the opportunity to get to know the younger staff who helped out there. They were 15 and 16 years old, but worked hard and played hard, volunteering their time to work in the kitchen, camp store and cleaning bathrooms all summer long. They were a great group, but were not afraid to give me a little sass, and I wasn't afraid to give it right back to them. There was a time they were supposed to clean bathrooms near the basketball courts, but one guy was giving me lip about it, wanting to play basketball instead. When he finally started to move towards cleaning, he threw the basketball forcefully towards the goal one last time. When he turned around to walk away, the basketball ricocheted off the goal with such force that it came back and hit him in the back of the leg, causing him to lose his balance. My reaction was involuntary – spontaneous, loud laughter as if I'd never seen anything so funny. It was like a movie being played out in front of me, when the obnoxious kid gets his comeuppance. I told everyone I saw about it, and I don't think he gave me quite so much lip again.

In between the work that didn't really feel like work most days, my friends and I made time for bonding. We had girls' nights complete with such giggling and hysterical fits of laughter that we probably kept the entire camp awake. The camp director always walked in at really inopportune times – like after a friend spilled salsa in her lap, making it look like she wet herself, then ran straight into the door jam trying to make a smooth exit to go change clothes. There were pool parties and trips to Waffle House. There were late-night candy deliveries to counselors, and tie dying underwear, including a pair of the camp director's (given to us by his wife, Nicole). These memories were like the logs of a log cabin, laid on top of each other, interconnected and strong, making camp feel more and more like home, more and more like what I wanted to spend my life doing.

Nicole led Bible studies for the Senior Staff girls, and we gathered together late, after everyone else had retreated to their cabins for the night. We ate junk food and watched Beth Moore videos and closed the night by sharing prayer requests and praying together. Sometimes we cried out of exhaustion or because the weight of the camp world felt like too much, and no camp season is complete without a few breakdowns when you reach the end of yourself. Most of the time we were thankful to be together, able to decompress in the safety of the director's cabin, sharing our needs and thoughts after leading campers and staff all day. We prayed for each other personally and for the counselors and campers under our care. We prayed for safety and for God to continue to move. Nicole always made us stand up and hold hands while we prayed, so we wouldn't fall asleep. Those times are that much sweeter because of the bond of standing in a circle together as we shifted our weight back and forth, ready to go to bed, but not wanting to rush the process. I have no doubt many spiritual wars were waged and won because of those prayers spoken by the women gathered together pouring out our last bit of energy before sleep.

All during girls nights and setting up games, I kept thinking about how I didn't want this summer to end. As the summer weeks went by, my fingers were ever so slowly releasing the grip I held on the camp experience. It was partly due to the tiredness that settles in at about week four, but also God was aligning my heart with His plans. However, I wasn't totally ready to let camp go, so I continued to ask God for closure and clear direction on my next steps.

During the last week of camp I was setting up the giant slip 'n slide on the field with some fellow staff. It was a perfect day with no humidity, brilliant blue sky, and a few of the big, white, puffy clouds that I love so much. It was the kind of day you just want to stay in forever. It was perfect, and I wanted to drink it in. Sitting at the top of the hill overlooking the field, I felt God speak to my heart. He told me this summer job at camp was the experience I had always wanted. When I had thought about being a camp counselor, having no idea what that even entailed, this was it. It was so much better than I had ever thought possible. It truly had been a gift from God – full and complete and amazing. I felt the closure I had asked for settle in and peace came with it.

I left that hill feeling confident I had received the answer to my prayer of being able to move on and also so thankful, so in awe of how good God had been to me. He had given me the greatest gift in giving me summers at camp. He knew how much I would love it long before I knew. He led me there one summer then brought me back again for two more, building friendships and deepening my love for ministry, for mountains and for Himself. He didn't have to do that. He didn't have to reveal Himself and His plan for my life in that way, but in his goodness, he laid it out before me like setting out a gorgeous picnic for me to enjoy.

A few days after I sat on that hill, as everyone prepared for the end-of-summer banquet, I was riding in the car with Jen and the song "I Could Not Ask For More" by Edwin McCain came on the radio. I knew for a fact that this song was not about summer camp, but since it isn't the Bible, I didn't feel bad taking the lyrics out of context. I really could not have asked for more in these past three summers. The words of that song applied to how I felt in that moment, not about a person, but about an experience. I knew it was God's way of reminding me that He had known all along what camp would mean to me. I smiled as I thought about how God showed His heart through a love song on the radio.

The following winter, I was back at camp working a weekend retreat. I sat up in the high ropes course, watching two high school boys race across the wires and logs, laughing and pushing themselves as only high school boys do in high places. They were bringing up the rear, following several kids who were nervous and shaking, but who overcame their fears for the sake of the high ropes course experience. I sat there watching them laugh and swing from element to element, and my heart felt like it could burst. I wanted this to be my life so badly. I loved watching the teens who overcame fears and pushed through the uncomfortable and the ones who enjoyed every minute of being 40 feet in the air. I couldn't imagine anything more perfect for me. My heart was alive, and this is what I wanted to do, what I needed to do with my life.

I graduated from college that May with no job prospects or really any leads. And even though I had an offer to go back and work at camp again for another summer, I turned it down, remembering the closure God had provided. Instead, I spent my summer trying to move forward, looking for jobs and trusting God would lead the way again.

WISCONSIN

It's a great thing to graduate from college. The freedom of knowing I never had to go back to school unless I chose it. What bliss! But with the real world looming and my apartment lease ending, I really needed to find a full time job the summer after I graduated.

I searched high and low for a year-round position at a camp and finally found a 15-month internship at a camp in southern Wisconsin. I felt I needed a year-round camp experience to make myself marketable as a full-time camp employee, and this seemed perfect. The internship mainly involved working with groups of youth, teaching outdoor education and leading them through high ropes courses and team-building exercises. There would be work projects and time learning to make maple syrup as well as discipleship aspects and a mission trip. I told my new boss that I wanted to make camp a career, and this seemed like an ideal segue from summer staff to year-round staff.

Anytime I told anyone I was moving to Wisconsin, they all said the same thing: "You know it's cold there." That's all anyone seemed to know about it, the weather. But I looked at the camp's website and saw the lakefront, and I pictured myself living the camp life in the beautiful setting. I had talked to my new boss at some length, so even though I had never been there, I was convinced it would be great. I just knew it.

The plan was for my mom and I to make the long drive north after a friend's wedding. The night before our departure we spent the night in a hotel room. Trying to calm my racing mind and stomach filled with butterflies, I turned on the TV and found a movie in which the main character was from Wisconsin. I took that as a positive sign! Then I opened my Bible to read about Abraham, who set off to a new land, not knowing where he was going, but just following where God was leading him. That was me. I was going off to Wisconsin, not having been there or knowing entirely what I was getting into. These were seemingly small things, but they confirmed to my nervous mind that I had made the right decision to take this job.

Mom and I arrived at camp late in the afternoon on a sunny August day. My new boss greeted us in the parking lot wearing Chacos, and I immediately felt more at ease. Mom and I walked around camp a little, took a little jaunt on the lake path and sat in the Adirondack chairs looking out over the lake that would be my home for the next 15 months. I held Mom's hand, something I hadn't done in years because even though I was excited for this journey, I was a little scared too. I said goodbye to Mom that night since she had an early flight home the next morning. And then it was me. I was there in my first job and home after college, ready for what the year held. Although it was new and a little uncertain, the familiarity of camp, even though it was a different camp, brought great comfort.

Because our house wasn't ready for us yet, my fellow intern, Keturah, and I shared a camper cabin for the first couple nights. We hit it off right away, finding out we had a lot in common, including but not limited to our love for camp and our excitement to find out what it held in the non-summer months. We told stories of the weddings we had just been in and of the camps where we'd worked before. After finding out we'd be leading night hikes with groups of kids – at night obviously, but with no flashlights – we practiced walking back to our cabin without any lights. We laughed nervously and talked loudly as we stumbled back to the cabin, imagining what was out in those woods no doubt ready to pounce on us at any moment. Those first couple nights in that cabin set the stage for a beautiful friendship.

After a few days of orientation, which included a canoe trip down the lake where I spent most of my time steering my boat in circles – not on purpose and not awesome – I settled in for the long haul. Most days that fall were spent with kids. They came in from the neighboring Chicago suburbs, and Keturah and I, along with other staff, played games, led them through ropes courses, and belayed them on the climbing wall. I learned and led silly songs around campfires, I taught classes on weather (which I'm not sure I did correctly) and played educational games about predator and prey. I loved it. The enthusiasm of middle school kids who were a bit out of their element was contagious. It was exciting to watch the kids try new things, and I was learning a lot of new things myself. I loved playing games out on the field until the stars came out, and living on the lake was a dream come true. I spent many afternoons in awe of the cool, crisp day and vibrant blue sky, which is one of my favorite things about fall. Even though our days were often full, everyday life at camp can be isolating, especially living in such a small town. The schedule varied so much that getting plugged in anywhere outside of camp was nearly impossible. I visited churches and Bible studies, but the only real community I experienced was with Keturah and our other roommates. And because the other roommates had different schedules, Keturah and I became more and more thankful for each other, knowing that without the other, we'd feel, and oftentimes be, very alone.

Within the first several weeks of being in our new home, I suggested to Keturah that we keep a list of all the memorable things that we do that year. Big or small, if it felt significant, we added it to The List. We tacked The List to the wall of our bedroom and added to it often. Things like night swimming and baking adventures were obvious additions, but when our vague inside jokes went on it, we'd remind each other later why that had been important enough to add. That list became an Ebenezer of sorts – a way to remember all the things we'd been through. It made us laugh as we read over it throughout the year, and there were many times when the days were tough that I was thankful for that list of the good things.

It quickly became clear that this job, although fun at times, would not be easy in any way. Being on my feet, hiking around with kids, lifting, climbing, running, playing – it wore me out. And those were the fun days. When there were no groups of kids, we did many, many work projects. We laid wood chips on trails, cleared fallen limbs from the woods, and blew leaves from the front lawn. We painted our kitchen, cleaned the remnants of a raccoon infestation out of a cabin, and made beds and cleaned toilets on housekeeping duty. Keturah and I made ourselves stay awake until 9pm every night, even though our bodies ached and we were physically spent every single day. "We are young! We are in our prime! Don't be lame!" we would tell ourselves. But after such full days, there was just no way we could party into the night. When the clock turned from 8:59 to 9:00, we'd already be in bed reading or just waiting, and immediately turn off the lights and fall asleep.

Those long days coupled with the lack of outside community and unclear expectations of what those 15 months would look like made work hard. Interns always have the reputation of being the grunt workers – fetching coffee and running errands – and this was turning out to be no different. Although our "coffee" and "errands" were more like heavy lifting and setting up tables and chairs. We did the jobs no one wanted, and while they were often necessary to the overall function of camp, it was hard not to feel underappreciated or dumped on. My body and mind were pushed to the limit.

During the winter months, almost every day felt like a challenge. As my alarm would go off in the morning, I would complain to Keturah across the room, "I don't want to go to schooool." And she knew that meant I couldn't bear the thought of more manual labor. I would force myself out of bed, and we would give each other pep talks. On days we needed extra encouragement, we'd don one of the matching t-shirts we'd made to make it a "Happy Day." Depending on what jobs were assigned that day, we'd put on shirts we'd stenciled with inside jokes about work ("I heart moving tables" was a favorite). The inside jokes on our shirts kept our spirits up, even as we layered on sweatshirt and jackets over them. We knew, and that was enough.

The more ridiculous our jobs became or the more tired we became, the more Keturah and I relied on each other – just knowing we were in this together, that maybe we'd laugh about it later or add it to The List – was incredibly encouraging. As we would clear debris or clean up the woods, we would sing songs from our favorite musical, *Newsies*, or try to remember all the camp and Sunday School songs we'd ever learned. Anything to keep our spirits up as we lifted one. more. branch. into the back of the truck.

We did have some downtime over those months, and those times called for some small adventures. We ventured to sleep outside under the stars on a warm October 31st. I'm from the south and a warm day often meant a warm night, but in Wisconsin, fall is still fall, and October is practically winter, and sleeping outside on October 31st means getting cold. We lasted until around 5am when we made a dash to our warm beds. On nights that were actually warm, we'd crawl out our bedroom window and lay on the roof looking at the stars. We'd tell each other stories about childhood or high school and watch the moonrise and the stars go by. Those moments on the roof or the moments in the kitchen making quesadillas for the fortieth time – those were what fortified our friendship over those 15 months.

Inevitably, after groups would leave there would be a stray disposable camera with no name on it, so Keturah and I started the Work Camera Chronicles. We claimed the camera as our own, carried it with us as we did work projects, and chronicled our tasks. Any time we found ourselves saying, "This is ridiculous," we'd stop and snap a picture. This made our jobs infinitely more amusing – even if it was only for a few seconds as we posed for a photo.

The bond Keturah and I formed over those 15 months was a gift I did not expect. Almost every night I spent as in intern was spent in the same room with Keturah. We had grown accustomed to each other's presence, and there was comfort in knowing my partner in crime was right across the room. I got used to looking across the room in the mornings seeing her bed neatly made up, because she had been up for hours reading, running, being productive as I slept. I knew that she felt strongly about her dental hygiene and loved ice cream and snow. We checked in with each other about what we should wear each day and made sure we always carried the "three essentials" (water bottle, keys and chapstick). She knew I liked Nickel Creek and Starbucks. We got to a place where we just got each other, and it was so good to know we had each other's backs.

Keturah was not a complainer or one to gossip. She was so kind to everyone, always thinking of others and putting them first. She wasn't vain. She worked hard and never put in just a half-hearted effort. Her example challenged me to be more that way too. I don't think she ever confronted me about any harsh words I spoke or complaints I made, but her steady, even nature, her ability to put a smile on and push through, encouraged me to be more righteous, and more like Jesus. Although I would complain to her sometimes, she rarely joined in, which diffused my frustration – or forced me to call my family so I could really vent.

That's the beauty of living in community even in, or maybe especially in, tough circumstances. There are people who can encourage you to get up when the alarm goes off, who will sing show tunes with you when the day is long, and who will remind you that God is faithful, and He will bring you through it.

We stuck it out together through those 15 months, even though many people urged me to quit when it just felt like too much. Keturah and I ran the course together. As our time together wound down, we continued to add to The List, and started to get sentimental about our upcoming departure.

We did a lot of "lasts" – our last time out on the piers, our last picture with the red canoes, our last trudge up the hill from the office to our home. We introduced the new interns to some of our ways – how to keep the work from stealing your joy and your life. They didn't seem as into the silliness that kept our spirits alive, and that was more disappointing than I was expecting. I felt like Keturah and I had discovered the keys to the kingdom in our Happy Days and our gratitude shown on The List, and we couldn't make anyone else see.

At our going away party, The List was proudly displayed. Some fellow staff read through in amusement, but they didn't really get it, which was okay. It was for us, and we'd treasure it rather displayed or not. And so we decided that we would each hand copy The List for the other person, so that the original would stay in tact. We decided to hide the original in our house somewhere as a sort of time capsule for someone to find. We placed it in the back of a collage picture frame we had been asked to put together to leave in the house as a keepsake of that year's internship program. Keturah and I snuck downstairs on our final night to put the list in its hiding place. It felt sacred to leave that list of memories hanging in that house as we prepared to move out.

On our last morning together, all the roommates gathered in the kitchen, circled up and held hands to pray. I started, but cut my prayer short as I felt the tears form behind my eyelids. Despite the hardships of our internship, our friendship roots had grown deep. By the time we said amen, I looked up to see everyone's eyes filled with tears. We stared at each other for a minute, then solemnly hugged goodbye, unable to believe that our 15 months had brought us friendship so sweet.

A SPOT ON THE TEAM

Everyone dreams of landing their ideal job right out of college, and there I was, one internship in Wisconsin under my belt, at my first real, big-girl job at the one place I really wanted to be – the camp where I'd worked in college. (Some would argue that camp isn't actually an adult job, but I disagree.) I had been hand-picked for the staff team by Hugh, the camp director, the same director who I'd worked for in college. He hired me, along with my other co-workers (including my BFF, Jen!) right at the same time, most of us under 30, confident we could take on the task of running a summer camp. I could not believe this was going to be my life.

I was nervous at first about starting this new job, and yet also naively confident that it would be great, and I would be great at it. It helped that camp was a safe place and a fun place, a place where I was among friends and could truly be myself. There were certainly some early growing pains on the team as we each pushed and stretched ourselves and each other before we settled in our roles. There was a learning curve on how to communicate with each other, with parents, and with others in the business community. Even though it was my job to answer the phone, at first it annoyed me when the phone would interrupt my productivity. I had to learn that the people calling were the business, not an interruption. Our team had to learn early on how to address conflict with each other and not let things fester because of how it affected everyone on the team. (This one took me a while, as I am a conflict avoider. In fact, I'm still learning this skill.) There was a time our team sat together in a van while Hugh made us talk out our differences. There was clearly an elephant in the room and he wouldn't let us get out until we had all said what we needed to say. It was uncomfortable, bringing back cringe-inducing feelings which felt easier to push away into side conversations and mumblings under our collective breath. But when we finally got out of the van, the air was clearer and we could move forward as a team.

Learning all of these lessons took place alongside learning about each other. Our team spent long hours together on Tuesdays reading through leadership books, taking personality tests, and listening to sermons or devotions Hugh had prepared. Healthy vulnerability was never an expressed intention of this time, but I've learned over the years something Hugh no doubt already knew - vulnerability builds trust, which lays the foundation for a strong team - and a strong team was an essential piece of running camp successfully. About a year into the job, Hugh gave the members of the staff the task of writing out our life story to share with the team, specifically a compilation of happenings that brought us to that point in ministry and in leadership – things like childhood dreams and hopes and hard life circumstances, anything significant that molded us into who we were. We sat around a table in the dining hall one morning and shared our stories. I told of my love for kids as a kid – playing with dolls, thinking maybe I'd be a teacher, and then going to camps on retreats in high school, working at camp in college, and how that opened up a new world for me. Working at camp on summer staff was a common theme for all of us– it had been life changing, a pivotal point in our lives, leading us all to have a seat around the table that day. We all arrived on the full-time team living out part of our individual dreams, happy to be chosen. Our stories varied, but each was personal and raw. There were secrets and hardships shared that had long been kept under wraps. We cried as we told of disappointments with our families, betrayals by divorce, our deepest hurts brought on by the hands of others, but how God used those things to shape who we were in that moment. And then there were happy tears as we told of God's goodness, the way He'd redeemed those hurts and how we ended up sitting around the table with friends who happened to be coworkers, doing work that mattered. Our jobs were making an eternal difference in the lives of kids, and even though we came to that conclusion differently, that was the driving motivation in wanting the job we had. Getting up from that meeting, we all carried a piece of each other. The dining hall had been a sacred space for us that day, and we walked out closer because we were able to be vulnerable.

That level of depth wasn't an everyday occurrence, but the fact that we could go there with one another was encouraging and strengthening to our team and to me personally. We cared about each other more than just on the superficial level of favorite Starbucks drinks and donut flavors (although that was important too – Americanos and chocolate covered creme filled were the most popular). Knowing I was important as a person, not just for what I contributed to the bottom line, made me want to work harder. It instilled in all of us a team mentality that served camp well. I wanted to do well for the team, and each of us felt the weight of carrying a big piece of camp.

The original team Hugh hired that sat around the dining hall table sharing our stories after year one didn't stay intact. After two summers together, there were other job offers, budget cuts, and life circumstances that moved people on. But that team mentality, the familial way we had because we shared of our lives, had been woven into the fabric of the full-time camp team no matter who was on it. That was part of what made this job unique. We were a family of sorts, and everything about the job was personal. No one was making enough money for things not to be personal, but more than the money, everyone wanted camp to be the best it could be because we had all been so impacted by it. We knew the potential for life change – the way staff and campers grew in confidence, in relationships, and in their walks with God. We sacrificed our time, especially in the summers, and gave camp our all. The team believed in the mission of camp, and I believed wholeheartedly in the work I was doing. I believed it made an eternal impact, and seeing lives change each summer is a powerful motivator. I cared deeply about each decision. Our team argued over small things like the time off our summer staff should have or what we should name new programs, because we were all deeply invested, and each decision mattered to us.

Some things, however, required no debate because we knew they were essential. The spiritual side of camp was paramount, and we all valued the times we were able to teach campers and staff about Jesus. The team took turns giving talks and devotions to campers and staff. The campers came into large group gatherings at the dining hall, face paint from a game still on, although smeared now from the sweat, and about to experience a sugar crash from the candy and soda they just bought at the camp store. But then it was time to worship. It wasn't fancy or high tech, but that made it more special. The voices were loud, echoing off the wooden walls and seeping out the open windows. Even when the song was unfamiliar, still everyone sang. When the speaker, who was a staff member, took the stage, the other staff and campers cheered a little – not in a "you're a rock star" kind of way, but in a "we like you and are looking forward to what you have to say" kind of way. When it was my turn, just that little bit of encouragement gave me a boost and quieted the butterflies I felt every single time I stepped up on the stage, no matter how many times I spoke in a summer. And what a privilege to share God's truth with these kids. I gave talks on hope and prayer and the importance of learning what God's Word says. I taught lessons from the lives of Esther and Daniel and Jesus. Sometimes we watched videos, and occasionally I cried because of what God had done in my life. Plus, I was often exhausted and my emotions lived right under the surface as I spoke. It was a lesson in humility to say what I felt God wanted me to say, then leave it in His hands without looking for man's approval. I reminded myself every time that God's Word doesn't go out without its purpose being served. And even though by that point in the evening some kids were dozing off or completely spent, there were a handful that continued to make eye contact and nod or even take notes. Nothing I said ever felt especially profound, but it felt important, and I like to think it made a difference in the lives of some of those kids and staff.

Just like during my summers as a counselor, the spiritual side was the engine of camp, but the fun was the wheels. There was still so much fun to be had, despite the fact that I had a lot of administrative work to do. Dancing, surprisingly enough, was a highlight, and some would even say an integral part of the fun. It was mostly on the last night of the week and usually limited to classic group dances like Cotton Eyed Joe and The Cha Cha Slide, but was soon to be augmented by the Spontaneous Dance. The summer that flash mobs had just become a thing, I gave a devotion to our Senior Staff loosely tied to a flash mob video that had taken place in England for a T-Mobile commercial. I told them how this is what camp is to kids. It's full of excitement and wonder and the unexpected. Never wanting to back down from the challenge of making camp even more fun, we decided to make our own flash mob of sorts. Several of us stayed up late choreographing cheesy dance moves to a compilation of pop hits. When the music played at breakfast the next morning that was our cue to flash mob the fellow staff. The Spontaneous Dance was born, and it was a hit! We taught the dance to everyone at staff training, so we could surprise the campers on the first night of camp at dinnertime. Then all summer long as the first few notes of the song played, staff came running from all parts of the dining hall to participate in the dance. We all danced and laughed and cheered as the song ended, then resumed life as normal - washing dishes, clearing tables, eating our chicken. And each time the Spontaneous Dance music played, more and more kids joined in, encouraged by their counselors to get up and dance, because that's what you do at camp when the walls start to crumble. The Spontaneous Dance lived on for the rest of my summers, becoming a beloved tradition that never lost its excitement – at least not in my mind.

The element of surprise was an aspect of camp I loved and wanted to implement whenever we could, whether in dancing or any other avenue. One summer we were going to give away REI backpacks to campers who re-registered for the next summer, and Hugh knew that if we gave these backpacks to staff, campers would be more excited to re-register in order to receive them. As we talked about the packs, the staff oohed and ahhed, asking how they could get one. "It isn't possible," we said. "They are reserved for the campers." And then during one training session as I explained how the campers could receive them, I said we'd decided to give out one backpack to a staff member, the lucky winner. We passed out envelopes with sheets of paper inside telling them the winner would have a picture of the backpack in their envelope. When everyone had one, the staff opened the envelopes all at the same time only to discover everyone had a picture. I channeled my inner Oprah yelling out, "You get a backpack! You get a backpack! Everybody gets a backpack!" while Jen and Hugh threw backpacks to the staff. Excitement rippled through the room as the staff realized what was happening. It turned to a bit of pandemonium as they clamored for the extravagant gift. Everyone screamed in excitement and, no doubt spurred on by the ridiculous enthusiasm of each other, continued to scream and laugh until the room was full of the happiness of Christmas morning and brand new backpacks for everyone. I smiled about that moment for weeks, remembering the euphoria brought about by a simple surprise.

It was these small moments, like handing out backpacks or leading games on the pool deck, that spurred me on year after year. At the beginning of every summer, when the staff arrived full of nervous jitters and excitement about what was to come, we all gathered on the pool deck before our first dinner together. The late afternoon sun was still hot, and everyone would migrate towards the shade, wishing they had remembered sunglasses. I led icebreaker games, and as the staff cheered for the Rock Paper Scissors Champion or tried to build the tallest tower out of shoes, my heart felt so alive. This is what I was made for; this is what I was meant to do.

Even the administrative parts of my job fit me. My primary job was to communicate with parents, handling camper registrations, emails and copious amounts of phone calls, among many other things. There were frequent times in the flurry of activity of the office when the phone rang nonstop, the copier jammed, and several staff were waiting to see me, that I felt the rush of doing my life's work, something carved out of the workforce just for me. It wasn't all fun, mind you. Like any job, there were things I had to do that were not my favorite. I folded and sealed a lot of letters for mailings. I washed dishes and put together staff manuals. I cleaned a lot of cabins, plunged a few toilets, took countless bags of trash to the dumpster, and moved chairs and tables in and out of the dining hall over and over in order to sweep and mop the floor, saying, "If I had a nickel for every chair I moved out of here, I'd be a very rich woman." Those were things in everyone's job description. We were all in it together, and if the work was going to get done, it was up to our small team to make sure it happened. The team mentality, of course, continued to be part of the appeal. Work was so much better when friends were in the next room, ready to help or give an encouraging word, and so it was difficult when these friends who I'd worked so closely with and shared my life with had to move on.

After four years on the camp team together, it was Hugh's time to leave. Even though others had left before him, he was our boss and in a lot of ways it felt like he was the glue that held camp and our team together. He was the driving force behind a lot of the team building and the cohesiveness our team experienced. He had been so influential in my life, always quick with an encouraging word or hug or advice, and obviously so influential at camp – the vision caster, the "work until the work is done" guy, the one spurring on new ideas. I wasn't sure I wanted to stay on after he left, as I just couldn't picture being at camp without him. He'd been a close friend and mentor and had impacted me in so many ways personally and professionally. He showed me what it looked like to love people extravagantly, and he reminded my task-oriented self that people were priority numero uno.

As the day of his departure approached, I told Jen about my feelings of maybe wanting to leave my job. She asked me once, as we were moving chairs into the dining hall from the porch –again – to please not leave camp too. I certainly hadn't made any concrete plans to go anywhere, but I just wasn't sure what I wanted. "I won't leave until God tells me to leave," I promised. I'm not sure Hugh was privy to this conversation, but he always seemed to know everything that was going on at camp one way or another. And before his last day, he came into my office to see how I was feeling about his upcoming departure (which was quite sad and confused). I told him I didn't know if I wanted to still work at camp, even though it had been such a rich season. He closed the door to my office and drew a cross in pencil on the wall behind the door. "I can't be the reason you work here," he said as he pointed to the cross. "You have to do it for Jesus. Because kids need to know about Jesus." I nodded silently through tears. He was right. Of course he was right. It had been short sighted to think that I would work at camp only for a certain director. I had to keep the bigger picture in mind – this is what I had been called to and this was what I was meant to do. Hugh's departure was an obstacle to overcome, but not a reason to give up on this job altogether. And so I stayed at camp. For five more summers I stayed, outlasting everyone else on the original team. That surprised me honestly, because as much as I loved camp, I thought others on the team loved it more.

But over the years of decision-making and sacrifice, dancing and laughing, surprises and the doldrums, camp became mine in a way. I felt ownership of all of it - the programs, the land, the people - and it held a familiar place in my heart that could only be earned through the intense amount of time and experiences had there. I fell in love with camp in the beginning, but even after the feelings of love faded, I put in the hours of work required to keep the flames stoked. There were a lot of hard days in those five years, mixed in with so many good days, and I often found myself looking at that pencil-drawn cross, remembering the bigger picture and thanking God for my spot on the team.

TREK TO CHOQUEQUIRAO

Somehow when planning vacations or being on vacation I overestimate my physical fitness. There were three vacations in a row where I ended up riding bikes – across the Golden Gate Bridge, around Acadia National Park, and through Seattle parks. And I'm not sure why they say, "it's just like riding a bike," as in, you'll pick it right back up, because all three of those times I struggled -with balance, with spatial awareness, with energy. In fact, in Seattle I actually hit a dog with my bike pedal. (It ran out in front of me, and the bike was too big and didn't have great brakes, okay?) Now, I would say I'm fairly coordinated and not a bump on a log, but when it comes pushing myself physically, I don't really like to do it, especially when other more fit people are present.

So when Jen and I, along with our friend Rachel, started planning a trip to Peru, I maybe should have considered a little longer the backpacking quest Jen had in mind. In a moment of weakness - or bravery, I'm still not sure which - I decided that I could do a trek, a multi-day hike through the

Andes. Me, who doesn't really like backpacking or overexerting myself physically. Sure! I'm game! I'm fun! I'm up for adventure! I knew it would be memorable, and I easily get swept up in the romanticism of the memories and the idea of once in a lifetime adventure.

When talking about hiking in Peru, Machu Picchu and the famous Inca Trail is always an option. But we kept reading about how busy it always is, how there are so many tourists and so little feeling of being off the beaten path, but rather a path that is well-beaten by everyone and their mother. So Jen talked to some friends who had lived in Peru for a while, and they suggested a trek to Choquequirao – lesser-known Incan ruins that hadn't been fully excavated, although it was believed to be larger than Machu Picchu. So with that recommendation and because I was brimming with optimism of my fit, vacationing self, we booked a four-day, 64-kilometer hike to the ruins of Choquequirao.

In the month or so leading up to our trip, I exercised consistently, but mostly pushed away the negative thoughts of "what am I getting myself into?" I could easily get myself worked up into a tizzy about how hard this might be, but I wanted to enjoy the whole trip, and not worry about the trek prematurely. I did the research, read the website with the description of the hike, and although it was certainly daunting, it was doable, I thought. It was only four days after all. I could hike for four days, right? Plus, Jen's enthusiasm was contagious. She was encouraging and reassuring that it would be fun!

Our trek left from the city of Cuzco and upon our arrival, we went to the expedition office to make our final payment and get any last minute tips. The owner of the company looked skeptical as Jen, Rachel, and I stood before him. Did he doubt our physical prowess? I mean, I did, but how dare he! He told us we needed trekking poles (he would rent some to us) and to be ready to go at our hostel at 4am. We would get picked up.

I'm not sure I slept at all that night. I tried to calm myself, talk myself into sleeping well, knowing that our 3:30 a.m. wake up call would be way too early. I needed rest, especially in preparation for our adventure. We got up in the wee hours, quietly packed the remainder of our supplies in our backpacks, and headed downstairs in the silence of night to meet our trek leaders outside. We passed through the inner courtyard of our hostel run by nuns to the big, metal main doors that led into the lobby, ready to step out and meet our guide, but we found the doors locked. That was unexpected. Searching around quickly for another door to the outside, we discovered there was not one. Unbelievable. The building doubled as a school, and presumably for security, it was enclosed with only the one exit we could find. It was closing in on 4 a.m., the agreed upon meeting time, and we could not get out of our hostel. In all our planning, we had not accounted for this. It was quiet and dark, the party going on outside late into the night finally quiet. Now what?

Jen had a phone number for someone from the trekking company, although we were unsure who. We found a phone in a common area of the hostel and called that number several times, letting it ring and ring and ring before we finally decided no one was going to answer (sorry for that wake up call!). Jen, forever the optimist, suggested someone climb out the second-story window of our bedroom, but there were bars blocking our way. What if our guide was outside, thought we weren't coming and left us? Although a small part of me was okay with that, I knew in the end that would be very disappointing, especially after all this build up.

After a few minutes of brainstorming, trying to keep our cool, we came to our last resort. There was a window in the stairwell, just out of reach, that we hoped led out to the front of the hostel. Jen volunteered to be hoisted up, offering to climb out the window, then lower herself down to meet our guides. Other than the obvious, our only obstacle was a statue of Mary, mother of Jesus, hanging just below the window. It was slightly dangerous, very inconvenient, and not what my cautious, over analyzing self would do, but we were running out of options and time. Just as we were plotting the removal of Mary, we heard someone coming down the hallway. A nun. We were saved! I tried to explain our situation in broken, 4 a.m. Spanish the best I could, and she took us to the exit, banged loudly several times on the metal doors, and the sleepy security guard who was stationed in the lobby let us in, or out, as the case may be. Crisis averted.

Turns out, our guide was running late (no surprise), and we hadn't missed our chance at this 64-kilometer hike. A black, king cab truck pulled up with four men inside. They got out and greeted us with smiles, loaded our belongings, and the three of us trekkers got in the backseat. Our guide, Milthon, sat in front with the driver, and the two other men rode in the bed of the truck with the stuff – for four hours through the cold mountain air - to our destination.

I tried to sleep some, but the excitement of the morning and discomfort of being in a strange vehicle headed to an unknown Peruvian location made it difficult. I was going to be fine, right? These men didn't just take our money to drop us off in the middle of nowhere. I tried to assuage my own fears, get comfortable in the back seat, and rest up. I had already been praying for this trip to go well, but as the sun came up over the mountains and I could see what travel conditions we were dealing with - curvy, narrow roads with huge drop offs made scarier by our driver ignoring any traffic laws - I upped my prayer game a little. "God, please protect us as we travel. And when we get there. And while we're hiking. Don't let us die." I may have been a little delirious from lack of sleep, but I still felt peace.

After a long four hours and a quick stop for breakfast we made it to our destination, the town where our trek would begin. We found out we'd be hiking with Milthon, our guide, and most of our stuff would be carried on donkeys and led by two men, our porters, Zacarias and Gregorio. The trek company owner and his teenage son would also be hiking at the same time, although at their own pace, well ahead of us. The scenery around us was beautiful. The town was tiny, reminiscent of a brighter Old West – only one or two streets with a yellow church, a school and a few colorfully painted, small houses. Right down the road was farmland, dotted with a few more houses. The majestic Andes rose in the distance and somewhere between us and those jagged peaks lay the mystery that was the road to Choquequirao.

The hike started off slowly. Milthon pointed out different flowers and trees. He knew the history of everything in the area it seemed, and he spoke fluent English (and French, we later found out) with an Australian accent. After less than an hour on the trail our porters passed us, prodding the donkeys along, moving at a pretty good clip, especially compared to our leisurely pace. We passed through a residential area with a few more houses amidst the fields, one of which proudly flew a small yellow flag. We found out that signified that they had *chicha* (corn beer) for sale there. Milthon called out to the homeowner who invited us in to a small room, barely big enough for the four of us. She dipped a glass into a five-gallon bucket of a strange, brownish liquid. Cheers! Rachel, Jen, and I each took a sip of the questionable beer made from corn, and that was more than enough. It was nothing like any beer I had tasted before - bitter and hard to swallow, especially because it was warm. Milthon thoroughly enjoyed his beverage and told us that many older men will regularly drink 8 to 10 *chichas* before lunchtime. That's not normal, we said. That's called alcoholism in the States. Our humor was lost on him.

We quickly discovered that although Milthon spoke fluent English, sarcasm and jokes did not translate well. We cracked ourselves up often, but barely got a smile out of him. I think he liked us. I mean, how could he not? But he did not get our jokes. Unfortunate for him, really.

The first part of the hike only had small inclines, and then flattened out for quite a while. We followed the wide dirt road as it hugged the side of a mountain, admiring the rugged, snow-capped peaks off to our right. We were creeping deeper into the mountains slowly, and I thoroughly enjoyed that flat portion on that road. Milthon continued to point out interesting things – agave plants, the remains of a landslide – and we taught him the beauty of jumping pictures. As it neared lunch time, we rounded the corner and there sat the cutest sight: a small table with a red tablecloth set up in the shade by a stream. There were our donkeys, tied up by our porters who had made us lunch complete with a stellar view of the Andes. We washed our hands with soap the porters provided for us in the trickling stream, and sat down at our table, our knees up by our chest in the short chairs, just in time for a herd of cows to pass us by.

I could get used to this – a little walking in the morning, with a picnic lunch just around the bend, although I had an inkling that our hike wouldn't stay that easy, and I was so right. That afternoon, we started our descent into the valley below. Long, dusty switchbacks would lead us to the valley floor, where we would cross a river before heading up the other side. The dust caked on my legs and turned to mud as it mixed with the sweat dripping down every part of my body. Other than the heat, I actually didn't mind the downhill portion of that day, except I knew going down meant having to go back up tomorrow. I pushed away thoughts of the uphill climb, and instead focused on the picturesque scenery surrounding us and the trail right in front of us. It was a long way down on one side of the trail if you were to fall (signs warned us not to lean, with pictures depicting a person falling), so better to pay attention, stay present, focus on the task at hand.

Late that afternoon we reached our first campsite, a green oasis of trees that shaded us from the setting sun. Our tent had already been set up for us by our porters and we were surprised to find out there were showers! Which we found out were "showers" with bamboo walls, which did little to provide privacy, and shower curtains made of tarps, hanging by a thread. Thankfully, no one walked the trail that passed directly behind those bamboo walls or they would have gotten quite the show - girls squealing from the cold water trying to stay as dry as possible while still rinsing off the grime of that long hike down.

The next morning, we were up before sunrise so we could get started in the cool of day. We didn't talk much in the first couple hours. We followed the lights from our headlamps while we continued to wake up, still focusing on those last downhill kilometers. The rushing river running through the valley got louder and louder the further down we went. The day before as the sun baked my skin, I just kept thinking how nice it would be to dip in that cold mountain river. As we approached that morning before the sun was all the way up, Milthon told us someone had recently been swept away in that river, hoping just to cool off. I passed on the swim; it was still pretty chilly anyway.

We stopped to take a picture crossing the bridge, but Milthon encouraged us to keep moving, to get as far as possible before the sun crested the mountains and the heat slowed us down. Thus began our uphill climb.
Jen said to me before the trip that hiking is just walking. That was supposed to bring comfort – of course I could do it, it was just walking. But that was incredibly oversimplified that day. Yes, we were still just hiking, - or walking - but climb felt like a more accurate verb. The trail had thinned into narrow, rocky, steep switchbacks. I was very thankful for those trekking poles we rented, as they gave me a little extra propelling to get my legs moving. The reality was that although I was hiking on those switchbacks, it was so painfully slow, I asked myself often if I was actually moving at all. My pace felt like a crawl, not because I wanted to be going slowly necessarily, but because I couldn't physically force myself to go any faster. I was so thankful for Jen and Rachel who never left me behind. They patiently waited at the top of each switchback, and seeing them up there gave me the motivation I needed to put one foot in front of the other. I had fleeting thoughts of "Am I moving too slowly? Is everyone really frustrated with me? Am I just an out of

shape loser?" I couldn't let myself go there, even though my insecurities longed to jump out and trip me up.

I read in Donald Miller's book *A Million Miles in a Thousand Years* that as he prepared to hike the Inca Trail, he kept Googling "Inca Trail, excruciating." For some reason, that kept coming to mind as I trudged up those steep cliffs. I spent a lot of time praying that day – praying that God would give me strength, praying that no one would slip off the side of the mountain or turn an ankle, praying that I would, in fact, make it to those ruins. I didn't really have a choice was the thing. There was no turning back now. We had already hiked a full day into the Andes, so I couldn't just sit down and wait it out. I had to keep putting one foot in front of the other, so excruciating or not, I was going to those ruins.

Partway through our uphill portion, there were sections of trees and the roofs of small houses peaking up over them. We stopped at one to use their hole in the ground toilet and to buy a beverage and sit for a minute. It was so strange to be a full day's hike away from civilization and find a man sitting in a hut selling bottled drinks out of a five-gallon bucket filled with water, attempting to keep the drinks cool. The majority of people who pass by that way are hikers it seemed. And there were not many hikers. What did these store owners do the rest of the time? Fascinating. Milthon chatted with the shop owner as we took a break. Jen was proud of herself for using the squatty potty. I was proud of myself for standing up after our break and making myself hike again.

The rest of that uphill hike was excruciating, indeed. My mantra became "one switchback at a time," just focus on the task at hand, just this one challenge right in front of me. We finally reached the top of the steepest portion in the early afternoon. There was a flat, grassy portion that led us to our lunch spot – a shelter overlooking the Andes with chickens running around. I've never been so thankful for a hot lunch, and I was amazed the porters arrived far enough before us to cook the very fresh chicken. Milthon gave us time for a little siesta after lunch, and we splayed ourselves out on the lush grass, soaking up the warm afternoon sun. At that altitude, it wasn't really hot, but just the right temperature for a cozy snooze.

My body wanted to be finished for the day, but we still had ruins to see! We hiked and hiked and hiked – the flat and downhill portions welcome, while even the slightest incline took all my energy and determination. By the time we reached the ruins late that afternoon, Rachel and I were spent. We took a picture outside the final sign pointing to Choquequirao. Jen is smiling brightly, feeling good. I have a half smile that says "I'm exhausted, but I did it!" and Rachel's is a forced "please don't take my picture right now" smile. This was Jen's favorite picture from the trek.

The ruins of Choquequirao were a wonder. The fact that they sat atop those mountains was the most impressive. There were aqueducts and farming terraces and structures still standing after hundreds of years. We only saw five other people at the top, and they were leaving the ruins for their campsite. Jen, Rachel, Milthon, and I had the whole place to ourselves. Jen took full advantage of that, hiking to every little peak while Milthon explained the history. Rachel and I sat down – finally – in the middle of a sunny patch and tried to keep warm while the wind whipped around us. I don't think I could've walked up another hill if I wanted to. I did take some time to absorb the scenery, even in my tiredness. I had hiked two days to get here, and I wanted to take it all in.

The river we had crossed so many hours earlier was glistening in the last bit of sunlight way down in the valley. The moon was already showing in the sky, even though there were still hours of daylight left. We were on top of a mountain, a mountain that I had climbed with my own two legs, one excruciating step at a time. A mountain that had seen a whole civilization live off its land and then disperse for reasons still unknown. How did they build this place? How much of it is still uncovered? It was surreal to be there, asking those questions, with my friends and no one else around.

At our campsite that evening, there were actual bath houses. I waited in line behind some loud French people, and again the water was like ice. It didn't feel as good that night since the wind was blowing hard up on that mountain top. Rachel wasn't feeling well, and even though all I wanted to do was lie down and sleep, I knew it was important to eat dinner, especially since our cook had worked on it for us. While Jen and I waited for dinner in the food tent, Milthon made Rachel some tea from herbs he picked outside. Was this real life? The combination of the cold shower and the wind made me cold from the inside. Even with the shelter of the tent, I was shivering. I brought my sleeping bag to the food tent and Jen and I got inside. During dinner, Milthon kept us entertained with stories of Peru. This was why I hiked for two days. I wanted this cultural experience. I wanted to hear the folklore and the history from a Peruvian. I wanted to feel the wind whip and see the millions of stars. I wanted to experience this with my friends.

We got up early again the next morning to start heading back. I knew the beginning of the hike would be downhill – so welcome after the day before, but then there would be some uphill too. There was so much joy that came from knowing we were halfway finished. This hike was so much more challenging than I was bargaining for, but also such a unique experience, something I knew I would not forget. We completed our downhill portion with no real problems that morning, but we started going uphill again as the sun rose higher in the sky. There was no shade (*sombra* had become a favorite word, along with *plano* which means flat), and I tried to hide behind thin trees with no leaves to get some relief. Sweat dripped off every part of me. My mouth was parched and my body wanted to succumb to the tiredness and just sit down. Milthon encouraged us to keep on going, just a little further. One switchback at a time, we made it to the green oasis where we'd camped on our first day and where our porters were waiting with lunch. After eating, we again took advantage of the siesta, lying in the shade, which was almost too cool as the sun kept moving across the sky.

I was feeling reenergized after our rest, and we were told we just had a few kilometers to go before we stopped for the night. All along, Milthon kept telling us our bodies would get used to the hiking and it would get easier. I thought he was crazy – how could my body get more used to this, especially after only a couple days? I just kept getting more and more tired. But after lunch, it proved true. Those last couple kilometers almost felt good. We got to our campsite and I was so pleased that I didn't feel like I was going to keel over from exhaustion, I was almost giddy. Rachel, Jen and I laughed a lot that afternoon. We couldn't believe we had done this, couldn't believe we only had a few hours left of hiking the next day.

Our campsite was actually where someone lived. They had drinks for sale there too, but I got a peek into their house and I saw a mud floor and a mattress and a few other personal items. It belonged to a couple and their teenage daughter. This prompted so many questions for me. Did the daughter go to school? Maybe she was on a break. Their house had a beautiful view. Their outdoor shower, enclosed with bamboo, even had a great view, overlooking the rugged, snowcapped mountains that had been constant companions on our hike. Incredible. That night we made a final trip down to the toilet before we went to bed. I stood and looked out into the darkness and up to the sky illuminated by millions of stars. There were no other lights around. Nothing. It was complete and total darkness, and people lived here. In the 21st century. And they were happy about it. It was awe-inspiring, and so different than anywhere else I'd ever been.

The next morning, Milthon didn't have to hurry us to get moving; we were ready to be up, ready to get that last portion finished. We hiked again by the light of our headlamps in the morning fog. As it started to get light out, our porters and mules passed us by one more time. Our porters had been so kind – cooking for us, taking care of us. We found out later they had been concerned for us, wondering how we'd fare. It was nice that they cared – complete strangers who cared about our well-being out in the middle of nowhere. I knew God was with us and sent kind people to walk alongside us during this trek.

When we got to the top of the mountain, we still had several kilometers to go, but we celebrated like we'd won the lottery – or more accurately like we'd finished a marathon. We laughed and smiled and took photos – with real smiles this time. It was a glorious feeling. We set off on the last leg, Milthon walked way out in front for most of the time, maybe because he knew we wouldn't get lost or fall off the mountain, or he was tired of our jokes. Rachel, Jen, and I took turns leading the pack and lagging behind, lost in thought.

Our last surge to get to the shop front where we'd started was a tiny bit uphill. Jen and Rachel pushed on ahead, and I brought up the rear, unable to force myself to move any faster. When we got back, the company owner and his son congratulated us on finishing. They finished well before us, but they agreed it was very difficult. A broad grin spread across my face, and I let out a deep sigh of contentment, unsure if I should spread out on the cool, tile floor or jump for joy. I felt so accomplished, like I had just been elected into an elite club of Choquequirao trekkers – crazy people who hiked 64 kilometers for fun.

Despite my tired legs, there was adrenaline rushing through my body as I absorbed the enormity of what I'd done. I was so proud of myself for finishing, for keeping up (mostly), for pushing my body in a way I hadn't before. It was such sweet relief to be finished, but more than relief, I felt such a sense of accomplishment. I really can do hard things.

I found out recently there are plans for an aerial tram to be built, taking 3,000 tourists a day from the nearest road to Choquequirao in less than 15 minutes. My first thought was, why didn't I wait for this tram to be built before I visited? But my second thought was, I'm so glad I took the long way, experiencing the excruciating and the glorious. It was hard-earned, but every step was worth it.

BFFS

After rumors had been swirling on the internet about a reunion movie for the show *Friends*, I read that the creators of the show set the record straight, saying there was no need for a reunion. The show had been about six friends, going through the particular stage of life in their 20s and 30s before they settled down, when friends aren't just friends, but family. As I remember it, the creators said they were happy with how the show ended, with the characters moving out of that stage, now having families of their own. They were not, in fact, planning a reunion, but wanted to leave those characters where the show ended.

I never really thought about needing friends to be family since I really like my family. But then, when I got my full-time job at camp, those coworkers crept into my inner circle, celebrating birthdays, sharing hard days over ice cream, having me over for dinner, and being there in the mundane of everyday living. They did, in fact, become like family, and no one more so than Jen. And I didn't realize how much I had come to depend on her until our relationship started to shift.

Jen and I met at camp, actually, as counselors on the front porch of Cabin 1, several years before we worked at camp year round. That summer we found out we both went to the same university and had many mutual friends. It was surprising we had never met before with the amount of things we had in common and the proximity of our lives on campus. Surely we had crossed paths before, but had never officially met. We were buddies that summer, but not true friends until we both returned to our university campus in the spring semester, each having spent the fall semester abroad in different countries.

My friend group transitioned quite a bit while I was away, and I was in desperate need of a friend that semester. And, after Jen and I crossed paths between classes one afternoon, I was hopeful we would form a friendship that lasted. Jen proved easy to hang out with, quick to laugh, and it helped we had a lot in common, including our love of camp. We spent many hours practicing handstands, laying out on the grassy area between our dorms, and then quickly became confidants too. We had so much fun that semester we decided to live together at school the next year after my third and Jen's second summer at camp, where we also shared a cabin. That summer thankfully solidified that rooming together was a good idea, and also solidified my love of camp life. I was thankful to have a friend at school who not only understood, but also shared my passion for summer camp.

The year Jen and I lived together was full of the stuff college memories are made of – at least Christian college memories. There were late night ice cream runs, intramural football games (complete with a super attractive team captain who we wowed with our cartwheels and giggles), cooking dinners together, and talking about guys, friends and family. Jen and I hung out for hours and days and late into the night because it was college and we could. Over dinners and errands, between classes and homework, and in our apartment. We sat in the same places on our well-worn blue striped couch, talking about the silly and the mundane, the sad and the serious, sharing our deepest secrets and the superfluous details of our days. We shared our hopes for the future, and a lot of times the conversation turned towards camp. It had been a special place to both of us, and there was always more to reminisce about. I made Jen watch the end of summer staff video over and over to relive the good times, and together we made a goal to call all the staff on the staff list, just to say hi. (We probably called 15 out of 80, but they loved hearing from us!) We had had the best summer, and we imagined what it would be like to work at camp year round. What if we could work at our camp full-time? What if we could work together there? We'd sigh wistfully and laugh it off, thinking that could never happen.

But, much to our surprise, it did happen! Jen actually got hired at camp first, while I was still finishing my internship in Wisconsin, and I came on staff later that year, in awe that I was actually going to work with my best friend. Every single day. At camp. Wow.

It was then, over the course of the next several years working so closely with Jen that she became like family. We forged a bond like sisters, and I mean that in the best and hardest ways. We certainly fought like sisters at times, getting irritated and nit picking, but just like I know my sisters will still be family at the end of the day, Jen and I pushed through arguments and petty jealousy to remain friends.

Jen and I complemented each other well, and that made our friendship flourish. She's more gregarious, definitely an extrovert, more impulsive. I'm a thinker, quieter, more cautious. But we both like to have fun and travel and take adventures. Because we had the same work schedule it was easy to travel together, so we took big trips to Maine or the beach and weekend trips to visit college and camp friends. Our road trips were never boring to us. If we ran out of things to talk about, which was nearly impossible, we could entertain ourselves for hours completing crossword puzzles together or playing Catch Phrase with clues only pertaining to camp. We spent so much time together on the road and in regular life that we knew what the other was thinking with just a look or a slight nod of the head. We even started dressing alike, showing up to work wearing similar if not the exact same outfits, unplanned, of course.

Jen became my comfort zone. I knew I could count on her if I was sick or needed a ride to the airport or a wing woman for an event. If I needed advice on what to say or how to deal with conflict, I talked to Jen. She was just an office away and we could and would spend hours talking about our lives in great detail, just like sitting on the couch in college. And we actually cared about those details. We could encourage each other, pray for each other, and share each other's burdens. Jen was there the summer when I was so disappointed by a boy I liked choosing someone else, that as we sat on the porch of the dining hall, I put my head in Jen's lap and cried, leaving tears on her skirt. She let me talk her into applying for The Amazing Race (I thought we were a shoo in, but we never got called.). She threw me my one and only surprise birthday party. I helped her paint her new condo; she helped me hang shelves in my apartment.

There were tough seasons of course, times when we cried together every single day – over the death of Jen's roommate or hard changes at camp. And there were family disagreements and boy drama and occasional jealousy or hurt feelings. But we supported each other through each season, talked things out and moved on as friends.

It wasn't just about support or a comfort zone. We also acted as iron sharpening iron. We could tell each other the brutal, honest truth – in love, of course. We confronted each other about hard things and watched each other grow. (I often give Jen a hard time about "wanting to see people to grow," which seemed to be her favorite catchphrase when she told people the hard truth about themselves.) Jen loved people well, and she was a great example of how to put others before myself.

We spent the better part of our twenties together. We grew into adults alongside each other. It was a wonderful and unique season that I often took for granted.

Because we talked a lot about everything, of course we talked about the men in our lives, or the lack thereof, depending on the day. Jen had great patience as I overanalyzed every detail of a conversation I'd had with a guy I was interested in. And when a guy from her church started pursuing her, I listened as she explained all the reasons why it just would not work. I supported her turning him down, and nodded as she told me why she hung out with him again after that. We lamented about how he just wouldn't take no for an answer and laughed about how funny it would be if he was The One, because she never would have seen that coming. And then, slowly, he did become The One. There was an email and a phone call and a retracting of "nevers" and then they were dating. And almost as soon as their relationship began, I knew this was the end of all that I had known of this era of friendship.

In what wasn't my finest season, I freaked out. There were some tear-filled conversations, and an almost accusatory, "Are you going to marry him?" within the first few weeks of them dating. My emotions ran the gamut. On the one hand, of course I was happy for Jen. This is what we'd both wanted for each other and for ourselves. This was a natural next step. We were in our late twenties and had held out for quality men. And this guy, Jeff, was a quality man. When I was thinking about Jen more than I was thinking about myself, I was really excited for her. But on the other hand, I knew that if and when Jen got married, my life would totally change. I wasn't ready for that change. Not only would Jen be married, but she would most likely move since Jeff now lived about two hours away. It had always been Jen and Abby – we were two peas in a pod, partners in crime, the camp staff even combined our names to "Jabby" because we spent so much time together. But then it became Jen and Jeff. He became her person – the one she spent her spare time with, the one she hung out with on weekends, the first one she wanted to call. When I thought about myself, I was unreasonable, immature and jealous.

I tried to hide those ugly feelings with varying degrees of success. I wanted to be always excited and enthusiastic, but there were more than a few moments when I just couldn't muster it up. Jen getting married meant things in my personal life, my professional life and my social life would change quite a bit. Our lives had become so entwined, and it was so easy to just hang out with her. I did have other friends, of course, but I had relied so heavily on Jen for several years, that I knew her departure would leave a gaping hole. I began to see that my dependence on Jen was not healthy and not fair to her, but I wasn't sure how to get out of that cycle, how to not feel sorry for myself or the state of our changing friendship. She was obviously excited, but she was also the one doing the leaving, doing the changing and the marrying. I was the one with the change being done to me, and I was not getting married yet, which was also a point of sadness for me. I always thought I would get married first. I was a little older, and truthfully, I wanted it more. Jen was content to work at camp and live the single life for a while longer, whereas marriage and family were high on my "to accomplish" list. Didn't God see that? Didn't He know that this wasn't how the plan was supposed to unfold?

While Jen and Jeff were moving towards marriage, Jen and I had several heart to hearts – her telling me that I needed to be more supportive and less negative, me telling her how hard this was for me. I didn't like the person I was acting like – jealous, petty, moody – and honestly, I didn't like the person she acted like – all couple-y and not sad enough that she was moving on.

Jen was set to get married in the fall, and to move shortly before that. We had one last summer at camp together. That summer was a tough one, mostly because of all those emotions swirling - hers and mine. There was a lot of good too, because camp is so fun, of course, but tough personally and interpersonally for me. Jen was emotional about her upcoming change of leaving camp, and I was emotional about the current change happening around me that I couldn't seem to get my head around. I was so used to always having Jen by my side at camp. We would get ready for bed at the same time and rehash our days, but that summer Jen spent many nights on the phone with Jeff. To me everything became about how it used to be or "this is the last time we'll…". I was so not ready for this change. We both cried at the end of summer banquet, possibly for different reasons, but both feeling the weight of the end of an era.

We took a trip to the beach for a few days after camp ended. We had grown accustomed to being together so periods of silence weren't unusual. But the silence on this trip seemed like such a waste. This was our last hurrah, and it felt like every moment needed to be filled with something meaningful. I realized that our friendship over the years had been meaningful to us both, and while we didn't need to fill the silence to prove that, I wanted to. I wanted this trip to be the culmination of so many fun trips, so many years together. Instead it was just a trip where we talked and laughed and spent time on the beach and at Busch Gardens, but it was just normal.

A week after we got back from the beach, Jen called to tell me she had gotten a job at Jeff's church, and she would start in two and a half weeks. Two and a half weeks?!? She wasn't supposed to leave for another six weeks, so this sudden move in her departure date was like a punch to the gut. I panicked internally. I wanted more closure, more time in the office together, just more time in general before everything changed even more. It felt cruel. Again, I was excited for Jen – this job sounded perfect for her. Of course she should go, and I would see her several times before the wedding at a shower and a bachelorette weekend. But, I was sad for me.

What I thought would be several more weeks of saying goodbye turned into two weeks of a flurry of activity. Jen was packing, still wedding planning, trying to tie up loose ends at camp. I tried to be helpful, wanting to spend as much time with Jen as I could before she moved. We said goodbye standing in the office parking lot after her sending off party with the camp staff. We said that of course we would still be friends, even though it would look different, and we'd see each other and talk soon. I didn't cry, although I thought I might. I had felt all the emotions times 100 already, so all that was left was to just say goodbye. And then she left.

After Jen left, my workdays at camp were quieter – my other coworkers asking me, "How are you doing?" with inquisitive looks, wondering if I'd fall apart right in front of them. During my lunch hour, I sat out on the bench in front of the office, where Jen and I had sat so many times together, and asked myself the same question, "How am I doing?" Of course I missed Jen – the camaraderie, the laughter, the lunch hour buddy – but I was also surprised by how fine I felt.

Although seemingly cruel at first, Jen's expedited departure date turned out to be exactly what I needed. I found that the anticipation of Jen leaving had been slowly driving me crazy. I had so many questions about what it would be like in the office, who I would talk to on my lunch break, how I would fill my spare time on the weekends, what would it all be like. And when Jen actually left, I could just go on living. I didn't have to wonder, didn't have to worry. I just had to put one foot in front of the other and live my life. She was my best friend, so of course I missed not having her in the next office. There were still waves of jealousy about her upcoming marriage and the ache of missing my friend. There's not a quick way to bounce back from your best friend moving, even in the best of circumstances. I had and still have some lonely weekends, times when I wish there was always someone to hang out with, someone who would meet me for ice cream at a moment's notice or watch a movie when I just didn't want to be by myself.

But all the ways I thought my life would drastically change, turned out to not be so bad in the long run. I had to make more of an effort to have plans on the weekend. I called different friends and spent time building new friendships. I came into my own at camp. Jen and I had always been such a part of each other's lives that I didn't always feel the need to open up fully to my other coworkers. Without Jen there though, I shared more freely with them and our relationships grew stronger. I was no longer one half of Jabby, I was just Abby, and I realized how freeing that was – to be my own self, to stand on my own and be validated as just me.

When Jen moved, our relationship got some space. While that definitely took some adjustment, it ultimately was much healthier. The close proximity began to smother all that was good about our relationship, but I couldn't see through the impending changes to be objective about anything. By the time Jen's wedding rolled around a few weeks later, I was genuinely happy for her and Jeff, excited to stand by her side and feeling much better about my own circumstances.

Of course there were still hard days, times when I wanted to laugh about an inside joke or give a nod to someone who just understood me. But Jen and I remain friends, just like we promised. We moved on from that tough season of transition and gained some perspective on life that comes from moving on and growing up and doing life differently apart.

THE DELUGE

At midnight on day two of our camping trip, Keturah and I scrambled for our rain jackets and headlamps and hurried out of our tent. It was pouring down rain, and we began to feel the water creep under the front of our tent, making it feel like a waterbed. We got out to bail out our tent pad, as if we were in a sinking boat– except the boat was our tent and the rain was about to overtake it.

This trip had started off so lovely. Keturah and I wanted to get together after not seeing each other for a few years. We had shared so much life in our 15-month internship and then living in the same city for a year a couple years later, but it had been far too long since we'd spent any real time together. We thought camping would be a fun adventure. We decided to go to a mountain lake near Asheville, and the campsite we picked was perfect - situated at the bottom of a few tiers of campsites, just a few yards away from the lake shore. There was hardly anyone else at the campground – enough people to feel safe, but no one immediately surrounding us. We happily set up camp, excited about the potential relaxation. It was the end of summer camp season for me, so I was ready to kick back on a raft or in my hammock with a book and not do too much for a few days. And connecting with Keturah again was bound to make for a good time, even though I wondered if our time together might be awkward since we hadn't seen each other in a while, but of course my fears were unfounded. We picked up right where we had left off, laughing, talking easily, enjoying each other's company – just like when we lived in Wisconsin.

The first twenty four hours or so of the trip were perfect. Floating around the lake and cooking over the campfire were breezy. We went for a hike and leisurely did the camping chores. I had jerry rigged some tarps over our tent and made a little portico, so if it rained, we wouldn't be relegated to the tent. We set our camping chairs under there, ready to read or wait out any bad weather that came our way. It was all going so well.

By the afternoon of the second day, however, the weather did not look promising. The rain started off slowly, the pitter patter of raindrops hitting the leaves, the lake, and our plastic tarp roof. It will pass, I thought, although there was an underlying sense of dread.

And then, the skies opened up. We scrambled around the campsite, trying to shove things in the tent, under the tarps, under the plastic tablecloth. It was really no use. The rain came down in sheets, soaking everything. We could sit under the tarp roof, but even the chairs we set under there were soon sopping wet. Inside the tent was dry, but we wanted to keep it that way, so we didn't go in. There was no escaping. The longer it rained, the more issues we had. The campsite we loved so close to the lake began to betray us. The rain ran down the hill and those top two tiers of campsites above us and flooded our campsite. The tent pad began to fill with water, unable to drain through the saturated ground. There was some faulty engineering there or lack of maintenance, but either way, we watched as the water puddled, creeping closer and closer to our tent. We wondered, with our rain jackets on, still getting soaked, how we should handle this. Could we dig it out for more drainage? And even once the rain stopped, we half-heartedly came up with a couple solutions that we didn't put into practice. We knew we needed a plan. More rain that night meant our tent would definitely flood, but something about being on vacation, not wanting to stress too much, we just hoped for the best. I should have known better.

I've come to expect a little rain on a camping trip. I had camped on many rainy nights before at camp and with my family. (My family had also spent much time at the laundry mat on those camping trips, drying damp sleeping bags.) And working at camp, it seemed our campouts were not complete without at least a sprinkling. There was one staff campout when the counselor girls, a coworker and I stood under a tarp for a couple hours while we tried to fix a collapsed tent and put up a sleeping tarp (and I will say, we got wet, but our stuff did not, so we slept out there all night – something I bragged about that whole summer). And for some reason it seemed I already had pushed aside the recent memories of that summer's rain-filled days, hoping not to relive the previous weeks at camp when it had rained anytime the forecast predicted even the slightest chance of precipitation. It had been the rainiest summer I'd experienced at camp, with so many rainy days, rainy nights, rainy weeks. The rain plan was never quite as exciting at camp, so it seemed we had lived with the perpetual let down. On the fourth of July, when there was no break in rain the entire day, I called the city phone number at least 12 times to check on the status of the fireworks. I wanted to go see fireworks, dang it. However, we ended up lighting sparklers in a pavilion and watching a movie with all the campers. Not a very festive Fourth. The only fireworks I saw that summer were from the video my sister texted me of the celebration in her town. So by the time Keturah and I were supposed to go camping, I should have been a little more mentally prepared for the inevitable monsoon.

The second night of our trip, despite our hopes and prayers for a dry night, it began to sprinkle. Normally I love sleeping when it's raining outside. It soothes and relaxes when I'm cozy in my dry, warm bed. But when I heard the drops falling on the roof of the tent, I startled awake. It got louder and louder as the sprinkles turned to an outpouring of rain. Keturah and I were both awake. "What should we do?" one of us asked. It was close to midnight, and I really just wanted to roll back over and fall asleep. But, we could feel the water puddling under the floor of the tent right by door. If there was any hope of keeping our stuff dry, we had to get the water away from the front of the tent.

We scrambled to put on our rain jackets and headlamps and quickly climbed out of the tent. We started scooping the water from the tent pad, but using our hands was not effective. "This isn't working!" we yelled over the downpour roaring around us. We looked around for something else we could use, and settled on the metal dinner plates.
Scooping water as fast as we could, we tried to keep the contents of our tent dry. Surely the rain would let up, surely we'd be able to catch up and get back in the tent and back to sleep. After several minutes of scooping, we realized this was

a lost cause. The rain was not, in fact, letting up, there was more water than ever rushing down the hill to our tent pad, and there was no way we could get it out faster than it was coming down. "This is not working!" we yelled, "What should we do?" We were half laughing, half incredulous at the situation, and despite wearing rain gear, water spilled down our legs, slipped into our jackets and soaked us. We stopped scooping the water to survey the situation as best we could. When you've been woken up during the night, then had an adrenaline filled few minutes of bailing your sinking ship while getting soaked, decision making is not an easy task. Our only hope was to move our tent. We un-staked it from the saturated ground and dragged it off the increasingly wet tent pad to a slight incline right next to it. It took some rigging, but we felt like we could get back in the tent and stay dry – at least for the night.

I know that rain is not a finite resource, but somewhere in my mind I thought surely it would dry up. Surely after a whole night of rain, there couldn't be any more left. But, as much as that makes sense in my mind, that is not science. And so the rain continued into the next day.

Because we had been warned of bear activity, we had been storing our food in my small car, which meant there wasn't really room to sleep there (although looking back, that maybe wouldn't have been so bad). The next morning,. we decided to drive ourselves and our food to a nearby picnic shelter for breakfast and to regroup.

We were supposed to be camping for one more night, but I was ready to pack it up. It was chilly and everything was wet, including several things inside the tent we had worked so hard to keep dry. There was no place to get dry and even if we managed to get dry, we wouldn't stay that way for long. Vacation is supposed to be fun, and this wasn't so much. I wasn't going to say outright that I wanted to leave, but I did drop some strong hints. Keturah didn't budge. She was in it to win it, and once I realized that, I decided we would do as we had done almost every day in Wisconsin – make the most of it, rain or shine.

We couldn't let some rain – okay a lot of rain – put the kibosh on our plans. So we decided to rent some kayaks and get out on the lake. We asked the park ranger if there was any hope for some sun that day, although I knew the answer before I even asked. "We're socked in," he told us. No end to the rain in sight. We rented our kayak, got out on the lake, and paddled around for a while. Lemons into lemonade, I guess.

For the next several hours there was unrelenting, continuous rain without even the pomp of a thunderstorm. No loud thunder or bright flashes of lightning, nothing to get excited over. Just lots and lots of water drenching everything. By that afternoon we couldn't take the dripping anymore. We got in the car and drove an hour to a Barnes and Noble. It was so dry in there! We ordered tea and scones and read magazines. It wasn't exactly roughing it like camping should be, but it was so welcome.

When we returned to our campsite that evening, the rain had subsided. The sun even came out a little bit – as if it was bashful after being hidden for so long. That night, we packed as much of our stuff into the car as we could in case of a rain relapse in the morning when we were supposed to leave. Then we hunkered down and cooked dinner over the campfire. We sat on trash bags since our chairs were still wet and chatted as the sun went down.

"No one tells stories about dry campouts," we said. Or at least that's what Keturah and I told ourselves several times, knowing it wasn't entirely true, exhausted after we'd fought the rain and lost. We had battle wounds in the form of wet sleeping bags and soppy towels, but we didn't leave early or abandon our plans.

And that night we talked about everything– our jobs, our lives, our hopes for the future. How we wanted to be married and have kids, but still wanted to have nights around the campfire with each other and with our families. We lay down and looked up at the stars and reminisced about all those hard days in Wisconsin and the nights we'd sat out on the roof, looking up at the stars there and having conversations just like this one.

There's a Sara Groves song called "Every Minute" that another roommate put on a CD for us before we moved from Wisconsin. That night made me think of the lyrics Sara sings about inviting friends on a campout with no other agenda but to enjoy nature and talk to each other. There's laughing and reminiscing and a reminder that friends are the good stuff in life. It's a beautiful song that I listened to over and over after my departure from Wisconsin, and it's never been for fitting for a moment than right now.

If we had gone home the day before or even that afternoon, we would have missed the best part of the whole trip – the night where the darkness stripped away the last bit of formality between us and we could just be. We could be honest and vulnerable and all that friendship is. Even after all the time we'd spent apart, Keturah was still one of my truest friends. I hope she knows that she's a friend I'm always inviting–especially when there's a rainy campout involved.

SINGLE IN SIBERIA

"It's like being in Siberia, really." Jen and I had been discussing the long, dry spell between any sorts of male interaction. "It's been so long, so dry and so hot. So, so long and dry," we'd said, conjuring up images of crawling across the desert, looking for anything to quench our thirst, our longing. "Actually," we realized, "It's not hot. More cold. Very, very cold. It's like freaking Siberia in here." And so when I'm feeling especially single or desperate to do anything to break me out of this rut, I text Jen with whatever wild-haired idea I have that I most likely will not follow through on and blame it on Siberia.

I feel like I've lived in Siberia for a very long time. Not for lack of desire to leave that cold climate – I've always wanted to get married. I wasn't a plan my wedding down to every detail girl, but I'm a romantic at heart, wanting the right guy to sweep me off my feet, kiss me under the stars, propose in some exotic way, live happily ever after. And I thought all of that would just happen in a timely manner – when I least expected it maybe, but definitely before my 25th birthday, and when that passed, definitely before turning 30. But here I still sit, and it's getting very cold.

I thought for sure I'd meet the right guy in college. Isn't that what people do? They go to college, and they meet their future spouse. Ring by spring and all that. I didn't go into college for the express purpose of the MRS degree, but I certainly wouldn't have minded that as a bonus. There were some great guys there – the one who flirted with me endlessly while he worked the desk in my dorm during my freshman year. I would count down the hours until I knew he'd be working and casually stop in on my way to the computer lab. He was so good looking and loved Jesus, and when my dad and I ran into him on a visit, he told my dad I was an "awesome, awesome girl." He made my heart melt - until the day he went with my "friend" to a baseball game. That sure seemed like he was on a date with her, and I cried for what felt like hours in my dorm room, feeling so betrayed and so passed over.

My senior year, there was the guy who went to my church who I immediately had a crush on upon first meeting. He was smiley and quiet and athletic. We were friends, always hanging out in group settings, but when he left me a voicemail the day after Christmas – just to say merry Christmas – I knew for sure we would be on the fast track to a happy relationship. But then he never asked me out. Incredible disappointment doesn't begin to describe the emotions I felt. We continued to talk and to flirt and on one random night out with some church folks in the summer after I graduated, we salsa danced. I moved the next day, feeling a bit of relief that it was over, but felt the disappointment again when he emailed about how he hoped it worked out with the new girl he was seeing.

There have been countless other crushes – as a camp counselor (what a great place to meet someone!), at camp in Wisconsin (there were very few men around, but I managed to have a crush on one of them), working at camp full-time (those guys aren't that much younger than me), and even, as a shopper (there may have been one small crush on the guy who worked at the J. Crew outlet store who flirted with me, but did not know my name. I saw him in a restaurant years later and accidentally waved. It was embarrassing.). There were guys I thought had real potential to be great husbands and guys I knew I would never even consider (except while in Siberia). But I wanted it to work with someone, more than anything I wanted it to work with someone.

The older I got, the fewer prospects there seemed to be and the more desperation seemed to take hold. Around my 26th birthday, a friend tried to set me up with someone from her church. We emailed twice, but nothing ever came of it, and I called my mom sobbing. She tried to gently tell me this wasn't healthy – to have this kind of reaction about someone I barely knew – but I couldn't hear her through the disappointment. Another friend introduced me to a single guy she knew, and I thought there was real potential. He was kind and friendly and spiritually mature. I only saw him once a week or so at a book club, and before each time I saw him, my stomach would be in knots. I couldn't think of one thing to say in his presence. My mouth would be dry, I would get tongue-tied, I would freeze up and act so unnaturally. I called a friend to pray for me once before I was about to see him, and she reminded me maybe it was best not to put so much pressure on things. Jen said that too – over and over – about Book Club Guy especially. "You're putting all your eggs in this basket, when he hasn't even asked you out. This potential relationship doesn't have to make or break you, nor does this one interaction. You aren't even being yourself because you're so worried about everything. Cool your jets." That was the summation of countless pep talks from Jen.

But I didn't know how to stop this weird cycle I was in. I wanted to be myself, of course, with Book Club Guy and any other guy for that matter. I wasn't exactly proud of myself for being so uptight, so laser-focused on being in a relationship that I could not even enjoy normal interactions. I wasn't trying to be weird or put pressure on things, but that's what was happening, intentionally or not. (As a small disclaimer, I wasn't acting like a crazy person with every single guy I met. I didn't do anything overtly weird or off-putting that I know of, but I didn't allow myself to be myself either, which hindered relationship growth immensely, especially with guys I was interested in.)

The truth was I wanted to be in a relationship that would eventually lead to marriage, which is not a bad thing – although occasionally it felt that way. But I didn't want to feel bad about that desire. I maybe could have handled the desire differently at times, but I felt like I had to play it cool all the time, that I was supposed to be content in my singleness all the time. Friends and well-meaning everybodies would give me the old adages, "Just stop looking for him. That's when you'll meet him. My friend So and So didn't even want to be married, she was so content to be single as long as the Lord wanted it, and then she met the right guy at Some Undesirable Location, of all places. My other friend took a break from dating from ages 18-21 to follow the Lord. She waited so long for the right guy, but then as soon as her break was over she met her husband. And another friend prayed just once to meet her husband, and then she did – the very next day!" I wanted to punch those people in the face. These quippy little tales were not how my life was going. I was waiting and praying. I hadn't dated enough to take a break from it, but I felt like I was trusting God most of the time, and obeying him too – saving myself for marriage, keeping myself pure and all that – but these things had not yielded the results I wanted. True, I wasn't content in my singleness most days, but I don't think that's necessarily the key to meeting the right person either.

The desire for a relationship was so strong some days, and it would pop up in the most unlikely places. Driving through neighborhoods, especially on Sunday afternoons when families were out playing ball or doing yard work, would make my heart yearn for husband and a home to share with him. Or anytime I found myself in Target in the middle of the work week, my heart would ache for a family of my own. Something about being in a store with moms and their babies when I was normally at work awoke the desire I'd held forever to be a stay at home mom. There were times when the desire felt overwhelming, excruciating and unfair.

It didn't help that it seemed like everyone I knew was getting engaged and married. Not just friends and people my age, but people I had known as kids and middle schoolers. Facebook would alert me to all of this (ugh) and my face would feel a little hot, jealousy rising up within me. "That person is getting married? Really? I have it way more together than they do. And I'm cuter," I'd add as a petty aside. "When will it be my turn?" I felt left out of a super-fun club – the club of wedding planning and home buying, couple's outings and God-sanctioned sex. And while I was being invited to weddings left and right, I didn't even have a date to bring to these weddings, which made me feel varying amounts of insecurity, embarrassment or sometimes shame.

I felt like I missed the memo on how you date and fall in love. Was there some class I was supposed to take? Is that why I have those stress dreams about being in college unable to find my classroom? Everyone seemed to be moving forward in the dating, marriage and family lane, except me. Mostly I could crowd out the lie that whispered, "There must be something wrong with you," but sometimes it snuck in and gnawed at my core. It must be me. It must be my fault that nothing ever works out. I must have some fatal relationship flaw.

The only thing I knew to do, the only thing I realized I could do, was to pray. Talking to friends about my singleness or the latest crush ad nauseum only added to my wistfulness. Not that it stopped me altogether, mind you, but more and more I took my thoughts and my feelings to God. I asked him over and over to open a door, to put The Guy right in front of me. There must be someone out there for me, right God?

And somewhere along the way as I sought Him, looking for answers about my singleness and about His will for me, He started to open my hands, releasing the grip I'd had on this desire.

I watched a talk that one of my favorite authors, Shauna Niequist, did at her church about Psalm 16. She emphasized verses five and six: "God has assigned me my portion and my cup, he has made my lot secure. The boundary lines have fallen for me in pleasant places." And as I remember it, she reminded the audience that if God has assigned me this portion and this cup, if this is the life He has planned for me, I'm not missing out on anything. God is writing the story of my life. He is the author and he knows what I need when I need it.

Of course, this talk wasn't the magic bullet. I still struggled to believe it, to believe that God's hand was in my life and in my singleness even, that he hadn't missed me or passed me over. But I would say it over and over through gritted teeth and tears, "God has assigned me my portion and my cup. He was made my lot secure. The boundary lines have fallen for me in pleasant places." And I would remind myself to keep my eyes up – to fix my eyes on Jesus, the author of my faith. I would preach to myself that God was the lifter of my head (Psalm 3:3). I posted that verse in my office and when I felt down I would read it over and over again, hoping it would take root in my heart.

God gave me more confidence in who He created me to be in this season – which is a single person, true, but He reminded me that is not my one and only defining quality. He showed me that my relationship status is not a determination of who I am or of my worth. Again, he reminded me that he was writing my story, and to stop looking around at the story he wrote for other people, but to keep my eyes fixed on Him. And when all those things added up, and when I remembered to apply them, I started to see growth in myself.

Slowly, all these truths became more of a reality in my life. I was able to see potential relationships as just that – potential – and not hold too tightly to anything right away. I even went on a few first dates with some guys who were fun and friendly, with whom I could spend a couple hours and then go on my merry way, happy to have had the experience, but not upset about it not working out.

Then I saw Book Club Guy at a party several years after we had met for the first time. He had since moved out of town near a city I was planning to visit a few weeks later. When I arrived, he was the first person I saw, and I quickly ducked into the bathroom. I needed a minute to talk myself into walking up to him and confidently striking up a conversation. I could do this. I had grown in confidence since our last interactions that had been preceded by an upset stomach and cottonmouth. I left the bathroom, made eye contact with him, and walked right up to join his conversation. He was warm and kind, of course, and we talked and laughed and then chatted throughout the evening. Before I left, I knew I had to tell him I'd be in his city soon or I'd regret it immensely. So even though I had to awkwardly wait for the right moment, with my coat already on, I let him know. "I'm going to be in your city in a couple months." I tried to sound cool and collected. And he gave me his number! "Let me know when you're in town." You bet I did!

When I visited a couple months later, we hung out, spending the day wandering through a museum and traipsing through the rain to a Greek restaurant complete with old-men waiters in white shirts and black ties. We had normal conversation, and I was able to be myself. He laughed at my jokes, and we had a really good time. I wasn't sure when I left if we'd be anything beyond friends, and as it turned out, he never made any moves toward me. But I was dang proud of myself for going for it, putting myself out there and being a little vulnerable. And subsequently proud of myself for not losing it in disappointment when it didn't work out. Progress.

I wish it had all been smooth sailing since then. I wish this chapter ended with me walking down the aisle because I have it all figured out. But, not surprisingly, my dating life hasn't been all uphill since then. There have definitely still been disappointments with guys (which apparently marriage doesn't cure, according to my married friends whose husbands are still people and still disappoint). I still get my hopes up and still mourn the relationships that have potential but don't work out, the guy who didn't call or text back in a timely manner, who didn't walk through the relationship door that was open right in front of him. I've shed a few tears, quietly and in private, when other friends have gotten engaged, but I have cut back on the snarky commentary and have mostly just been happy for them. The last couple weddings I've gone to without a date, I've made the choice not to feel sorry for myself, and I've thoroughly enjoyed them.

Even though I see the growth in myself, I still ache with desire at times, and remind God that I'm ready for a relationship and still single. Don't You see me? Don't You hear me? And in God's faithfulness, He always reminds me that He, in fact, does see and hear me. I have not been forgotten and He is not holding out on me. And, thankfully, I believe it more and more.

On my best days, I'm confident, sure of who I am and where I am in life, and perfectly content. And on my worst days I can still be a petulant child, wanting my way right now with the guy I think is perfect for me. But, thankfully, on most days I just live my life and try to trust that God's timing is perfect.

IS THIS DATING?

A few weeks after I started my new job, I sat on a Q&A panel for our dating retreat as the "single girl" along with "single guy," "married couple," and "engaged couple." People had submitted questions beforehand and the moderator, a fellow staff member, whispered to me that my next question was, "How do you know when you've found The One?" I was a little confused, because clearly I haven't met The One yet, but that question was coming my way, ready or not. I said something along the lines of, "I've really only known guys who weren't The One. I've known and even had interest develop with a few great men, who, had they asked me, may have made fine husbands. But I have to trust God will make it clear when I meet the right person for me, just like he's made it clear that those guys have not been God's best for me." It was a fine enough answer, one I wish I believed all the time, but often I fall into the trap of "gotta make it happen." If I don't do something about my singleness right this minute, then I will be single forever. This normally leads to desperation, which sometimes leads me to online dating, which is not inherently bad, but I think I've used it to cure all that ails my heart, which does not work (shocker).

Online dating is such a weird thing. It can be fun and it can be really frustrating. I've actually had the most success in my dating life from online dating. I'm not sure if that says something about me personally, but I'm going to choose not to read into it. I have learned a few valuable lessons from it though. First of all, never respond when someone you've never had any interaction with would like to use the "chat" feature. I've learned the hard way the social skills may be lacking. First I "met" the Interrogator who peppered me with so many questions I barely had time to respond. I wanted to tell him that this is not an interview, and just to give me a minute. Not to mention his fourth question in was, "What is your favorite Bible verse?" If we were talking in real life for the first time and the fourth question you asked me was about my favorite Bible verse, it would be odd. So maybe hold off on that. The second person I met by "chatting" was the LOL Guy. Possibly my least favorite thing in any online forum is the person using LOL superfluously. You are likely not laughing out loud, and if you are laughing after every sentence, I'm not sure we are compatible. The LOL Guy was very enthusiastic. He used a lot of exclamation points and reminded me of camp counselors with weird hats and jungle print shirts. This guy proceeded to tell me about the "funny" prank he was involved in the night before – something involving friends who gave him a wedgie and left him hanging on the back of a door for hours. LOL. I'm not sure if it was true, but it did not make me want to continue our conversation.

Despite the odd balls, sometimes online dating seems like the only way I'll ever meet a potential suitor. (I have a couple friends who have met quality men on the internet, and that has kept my hope springing eternal). And one time I did meet someone, and we hit it off. It was fun and honest and had potential, and I wanted it to work. His name was James, and I almost wrote him off before it even began.

James and I started by sending quick emails – short notes to get a feel for each other. "What do you do? What are your hobbies?" That soon turned into longer emails, asking lots of questions, "What kind of church do you attend? What's your family like?" Things that could be accomplished quickly if you knew each other or met in person, but alas, via the Internet, took forever. He was amusing and continued to respond in a timely manner, and when I found myself feeling a few butterflies while reading his emails, I knew there was promise. We continued to email about funny work interactions and our favorite stories to tell at a party, but after a couple weeks of witty banter and innocuous questions, I felt like I was slogging through waist-deep water in the amount of ground we had covered.

Since James lived in a different state, I knew we wouldn't meet in person any time soon, but I was ready for him to either move this thing forward or be done all together. So I started looking for reasons to write him off, of course. I wanted to be in a relationship, sure, but it wasn't progressing quickly enough, he didn't fit the ideal in my head, and I was tired of emailing. (I know, I know. Give a guy a chance). Why I'm looking for reasons to say no, when I really want to be saying yes, is a mystery. A bit uncharacteristically, I decided with James that I would continue to say yes to him until I found an actual, substantial reason to say no. Then I decided to ask some heavy hitting questions about God and faith and I was pleasantly surprised to find his answers compatible with my beliefs. And, just when I thought we'd be emailing indefinitely, I prayed that God will give him the courage to lead, and he asked for my phone number.

James called that night (!), and I was impressed he didn't feel the need to wait three days or play it cool. As you might expect, the conversation had its awkward pauses and overly enthusiastic laughing – but there was laughing on both sides, and that says potential like nothing else. I enjoyed talking to him on the phone, and I was interested to see where this would go next.

After that first phone call, James and I talked or facetimed a couple times a week for a few hours. Since we couldn't easily go on a real date, this was the next best thing, although it felt strangely intimate since through the magic of internet and smart phones, we could see each other in each other's homes. It was new and fun, and he liked me and wasn't afraid for me to know it, which was endearing to say the least. And as much as I didn't want to be "that girl" that got all googly eyed over a boy who liked her, I felt myself wanting to talk about him all the time, smiling more often and feeling a little spring in my step as I went throughout my day.

I was really enjoying myself and this new thing with James, but I had to make a choice most days to not freak out. We were having fun, but being a planner, it was difficult for me not to want to know if this was "it." I tried to enjoy each day, each text, each phone call for what it was. I'd tell myself not to read into anything, just take things as they come. Normally when I sense interest from a guy I immediately start planning our wedding (if I'm also interested) or I act completely awkward and stiff (if I'm not interested). I had yet to find the middle ground of letting things play out naturally, seeing where the other person stood and if he was someone worth planning a wedding over. So the fact that I had kept my cool in my head and in my heart with James was no small victory.

We talked or texted often, but at one point I stopped hearing from him for a few days. Maybe he lost interest. Maybe he's dating someone else who actually lives nearby. Maybe I will never hear from him again. Maybe I'm driving myself crazy. Not knowing why the communication stopped was agonizing, and because I felt very strongly that he was supposed to lead in pursuing me, I didn't know how to proceed or even if we should proceed. Was it ever okay for me to call him? And not just that, but I needed answers for other things too – was I being an appropriate amount of vulnerable? How is this whole long-distance, phone talking "relationship" thing supposed to go anyway? (No one has ever accused me of under-analyzing a situation.) I asked Jen for advice. I asked the girls in my office, and in a real vulnerable moment, I asked a married guy friend and coworker what he thought. What should I be doing? Someone just tell me!

After all my freaking out, I felt God's gentle guidance. It was as if His hand was on my back, telling me to chill out (kindly and lovingly, of course). There is no "supposed to." Everyone's relationships are different. And while I wanted validation from other people that I was doing things correctly, ultimately I had to just ask God. He was the only one who knew how this was really going and what I "should" be doing. There are no set rules of who calls when or what I should or shouldn't be saying. When I did finally hear from James again (he had been sick), I told him that I missed hearing from him. Maybe that was too honest, too much too soon, but I realized I had to tell the truth. I had to be myself and share myself, regardless of the "rules."

After a while, James and I started talking about how we could meet in person. It would probably involve a plane ticket and a little more of a commitment. I insisted that he come my way first before I would even think about going to see him, and we picked dates and talked logistics, and it seemed it was really going to happen at the end of the month for a stretch of five days (which I was slightly concerned about...what if it didn't go well, and we were stuck together for five days?).

One beautiful spring morning, a couple weeks before the time he was going to visit, I was at work at the camp office and got a call from the gatehouse announcing a guest. "You have a friend here."

"I do?"

"Yes, James is here. I sent him out to camp. I didn't figure you'd mind."

Oh. My. Gosh. "James is here!" I announced to anyone within earshot. The girls in my office freaked out with me for a moment. As a teenager, I had daydreams about things like this – the boy I had met at some out of town thing or the cutest boy in high school would just show up at my house unannounced (perhaps I watched Sixteen Candles a time or two). He would bring flowers and confess his like of me, and it would be great. I never thought it would actually happen. Like ever. But here I was, in what felt like a Hallmark movie, where the boy I liked had driven through the night to surprise me and meet me and spend the day with me. He even brought chocolate. Swoon.

Thankfully, I had a few moments to collect myself after the phone call before James actually got to my office. I checked the mirror, glanced down at my outfit (a skirt, a camp shirt – could be worse), paced a little. I greeted him outside away from the curious glances of my coworkers.

"What are you doing here?" I asked with a smile.

"I was just in the area," he answered with a confident grin. He came inside and met my friends, and we went for a walk around camp.

I "worked" for a little while longer, while James napped. I texted Jen, "James is here," and she texted back, "I'm freaking out right now!" Tell me about it. I called both my sisters who immediately asked what I was wearing. Then James and I went to lunch, where we hardly ate anything. I asked my boss if I could leave early, because, let's not kid ourselves, my productively level was at an all-time low. (My boss said "Yes, but do not fall in love," as a joke. I made no such promises.) James and I played Frisbee and putt putt and ate ice cream and pizza. There was some concern from my friends and family (who had been so gung ho about this when it was merely a phone talking relationship) that James was a stalker, but I felt at ease, knowing his character and his motives seemed pure. And it helped that he physically kept some distance, not trying to touch or even hold my hand. Bonus points for his awareness on how that may come across.

That night we sat under the stars talking about our feelings and our past and the possible future. We asked questions of each other like we had before, but it felt like more was at stake that night. This was the real deal. We were physically together, side by side, and I needed some real insight into who he was in the depths of himself if this was to move forward. The problem, I'd discovered, with meeting someone online from a different state is that there is no context for the other person. I didn't know his friends or his church. I didn't know what kind of food he orders or how he treats waiters. We had shared some anecdotes on how God had worked in our lives, but God wasn't a part of everyday conversation, and that kept nagging at me. Even after countless hours on the phone, there were a lot of unanswered questions. I got quiet a couple times thinking about the potential of this relationship. That day had been so fun, a little surreal even. The more time we spent talking, though, the less peace I had. I got nervous – like pit of your stomach, Holy Spirit check nervous – and I didn't like that. I blamed it on the late hour, because that can do weird things to my mood, but suddenly I just wanted to be out of there. I wanted to be home, sleeping and not talking anymore. I had this overwhelming desire to leave.

We parted on good terms, with a hug and a selfie to commemorate our day. I didn't let on that I was feeling nervous to the point of no return.

I lay in bed that night mulling over the events of the day, trying to calm down, willing peace to come, but even when I woke up the next morning I still kind of freaking out. "I'm probably just tired," I thought. After spending the day with someone I liked, who had surprised me no less, I should be feeling great, right? "Is this how I'm supposed to feel? If James is the one, shouldn't there be peace?" I asked myself again. I wanted to call in sick to work that day, even though I knew my upset stomach was from stress and lack of sleep. There would be questions from my coworkers, and I wanted to tell them everything was storybook perfect, the day had been all I hoped it would be, and I was on my way to happily ever after. But it wasn't true, and I didn't want to believe it. I called Jen on the way to work, expressing my concerns and asking her the same questions, "Is this normal? Am I just tired? This doesn't mean anything about James, right?" She gave me the encouragement I needed, but I fought back tears as I got off the phone. And later, when a coworker asked how it went, all I could say was, "I don't know."

Over the next couple days, after getting some rest, I started to feel more normal about James again. We still weren't even officially dating, so there was no need to decide whether I'd walk down the aisle with him or move to a different city to be with him. I could just enjoy each day and make a decision when he asked me to. Keep saying yes.

A couple days after the visit, I stopped hearing from James. My texts got short responses. There was still official "be my girlfriend" talk, so maybe he didn't feel he owed me anything. In my mind, however, an impromptu surprise visit, no matter how short, necessitated some kind of follow up. His lack of initiative felt so abrupt. He had been so forward, so forthcoming for weeks, and now nothing. Not even a call to say he was done. If he didn't want to talk any more, he needed to tell me that, I didn't want it to just slowly fade away.

When I sought advice from friends, it did not help. "He probably won't call. Guys just do that because they don't want to end things." "You should call him." "You shouldn't call him." No one knew the right thing, because no one else was in it with me and James.

When I talked to God about what I should do, I felt strongly that God was telling me I needed to wait, because he wanted James to lead. I cried about the unknown, about the loss of the potential relationship, about the loss of a phone buddy. Not surprisingly, the more I spent time with God, the better I felt. I was able to get out of my own head and gain some clarity. It didn't always stay, as I could talk myself into a tizzy pretty quickly, but when I allowed God to permeate my thoughts and feelings, I was able to hold the relationship in an open hand, something I hadn't been very successful at in other potential relationships.

Eventually, James and I talked. He had been busy with a new job and a weird schedule, he said. Even though I wasn't convinced, I tried to believe him. We did agree that it was time to make a decision on where this was headed. We decided we'd take the upcoming weekend to pray about things, and he would call on Monday. All day on Sunday, I sought God's will for this relationship through fasting and prayer. It seems kind of funny since we weren't even dating to be so serious about this, but both James and I were ready for serious. We weren't willing to date long distance if this wasn't going to head somewhere serious. After praying on Sunday, I felt I had an answer – that I'd be willing to try this out if he was willing.

But then when I woke up on Monday morning, I knew this relationship wasn't going to happen. Driving to work, I thought about my future, and while I liked the idea of being a couple, of having someone to do things with and talk with throughout the week, I wasn't necessarily excited about James being that person.

I waited all day for James's call, wondering what he was going to say, how I was going to respond. Would I still be open if he was interested, even though I knew it wasn't the best thing for me? The whole day I just kept thinking about how I didn't want to cry on the phone with him, not matter what happened. When he didn't call until 10:30 that night, I knew what the outcome of the call would be, and I certainly was not in a crying mood. I was just annoyed. We made small talk, and then he dropped the "I just don't feel any chemistry" card. It was a cop out and I knew it, but I didn't press for anything more.

As I got in bed that night, I waited for the emotions to come. I thought I might cry some more or feel really sad, but there was such a finality to it all. I knew it was right that it ended then, even though maybe it could have worked for just a little while longer, if not for the long haul. I knew James hadn't been God's best for me. I knew all those feelings of unrest were God's way of showing me His plan.

In the coming days, I felt more confident of the rightness of the situation, but also more disappointed in the loss of the potential relationship. It was strange to be so sure that it was right to have ended things, but still be sad to not have it anymore. James said he wanted to stay friends, but I knew we wouldn't. When a relationship based solely on potential ends, the friendship ends as well.

So I moved on with a full heart and no regrets – more confident in myself, more aware of the power of being vulnerable, more sure that God will lead me to The One when the time is right.

FARMHOUSE LIVING

There is a small window at the end of each summer when my family is all free. I'm finished with camp and no one has gone back to school yet. I get a week or two off to recover from my hectic summer schedule, and my family has enough time for one last vacation before the long haul of school begins. After an intense summer, I'm always ready for some time away with people who don't necessarily need anything from me. It's mostly easy for our family to be together, so the weeks we share are a treat for us all.

One year, my sister Erin found an old but updated farmhouse outside of Charlottesville, Virginia, for us to rent. I drove there from Asheville by myself in one day and, still feeling sleep deprived from the busy season, I could not wait to be there and relax. I followed the GPS to the address given, and even though it told me my destination was on the right, the long white split rail fence on the left gave it away. I knew from the long periods of time spent on the rental website, longing to be with my family, that the beautiful farmhouse sat back behind that fence somewhere. I turned left in the driveway and stopped to take a photo before I got any closer. I could see my family's cars parked under the giant tree on the left and the wide front porch was just waiting to be sat on.

I walked in the side door, taking in all the quaint details of an old house restored. There were wide planked floors, a giant dining room table, plenty of seating areas, several bedrooms with multiple beds. It was perfect for a family getaway. I found my family after wandering through some downstairs rooms and out through the screened-in porch. They had been there for several hours and had already been swimming in the pristine pool in the backyard.

There are some days when everything just seems perfect to me, and I've learned I feel that way largely when the weather is good. When the sky is blue, the sun is out, there's no humidity, it's 80 degrees - warm but not hot in the sun - and perfect still in the shade, a cool breeze, and there's green grass all around and even better when there's a mountain view. Days like that are made for living. I feel good. I feel alive. I feel like I never want to go inside. God feels closer, nearer to my spirit. It's like He has made that day just for me, just because He knew I would like it, would soak it in, and want to be out in it with Him.

That's how it was almost every day at that Virginia farmhouse. We spent the last of the long, summer days by the pool, reading, playing, practicing backflips and Dirty Dancing lifts off the diving board. I lazed every day, just enjoying the mountain views, the sights and sounds of my nieces playing, and reading a good book. I sat in the sun until it was too warm, then put up the umbrella for just the right amount of shade. I tanned and napped and only knew the passing of time by my hunger for lunch. It was even cool enough to enjoy the hot tub or the "hot pool" as my niece calls it. We'd get in and get out, too warm, then wanting to be warmer.

In the mornings, I'd go for a run or a walk on the country roads, breathing in the crisp air. There were farms and houses big and small dotting the countryside, but it felt like I had the whole area to myself. It felt good to do some purposeful exercise after the long summer of exercise that consisted mostly of walking from the office to the dining hall or to my cabin. It felt good to run, to breathe deep, to push my body again. And then it felt good to walk, to chat with my sister, to smell the flowers by the road.

After a day full of pool sitting, the family took turns cooking dinner for each other. We grilled out and baked, set the table for 12, and sat around relishing in each person's faire. Everything tasted so good, partly because we didn't make it ourselves, partly because being in the summer sun creates such a deep hunger, and partly because we really are actually good cooks. Those who cooked weren't allowed to clean up, so we'd sit around the table a bit longer, making plans for the evening.

While we waited for dinner when it wasn't our night to cook, we'd sit outside on the wide front porch watching the sunset. Or we played croquet in the side yard, letting sibling rivalry get the best of us as we launched the balls across the lawn wanting to win so badly. Each day and each evening were just picturesque. We sat in the hammock, swung on the tire swing, explored the barn looking for eggs careful to avoiding the resident snake, and watched the goats. We walked down by the pond and all around, pretending it was home and loving that it was, even for just one week.

In the evenings we entertained ourselves in different ways, and one favorite family pastime is always playing games-Yahtzee because Grandma likes it and we've been playing since we were all kids. And Trivial Pursuit because no family get-together is complete without some fierce question and answer sessions. It's a matter of pride, really, who knows the most about pop culture and history. I know it's not me, but I can occasionally come through in a pinch and at least contribute good, if sometimes uninformed, suggestions.

We found out there was a bluegrass band playing at a general store nearby one night. We drove on down, and it was just the slice of Americana we were looking for. The store had a hodgepodge of merchandise, seemingly more random than the usual general store. We bought sodas in glass bottles and took them out to the lawn where the band was already playing. We sat in creaky lawn furniture, the metal kind with flower cutouts. There were 10 or 15 musicians sitting on a low stage with a larger than life stuffed tiger sitting on a seat to the left of the musicians, presiding over the festivities. It quickly became clear this wasn't as much of a concert as it was a jam session. The musicians picked their guitars, banjos, upright basses and violins. As it got closer to 10 pm, they started packing up one by one, heading home. They wished each other a good evening with promises to see each other next week. We stayed until the last band member called it a night.

One night we wandered around taking pictures for our Christmas cards on the porch, by the split rail fence, walking up and down the road, enjoying each other's company and the setting sun. The golden hour they call it, that perfect bit of light before the sun dips behind the mountains. I love taking pictures to capture those moments. I like to be present and live in them too, so it's sometimes a hard balance. But I've found that when I look back on pictures, I can transport myself back to that moment, to the happiness I felt, to the way the breeze felt on my skin, the way the clouds scattered across the sky as the sun went down. Pictures allow me to remember all the good, all the fun, all the ways God showed up.

We decided that no trip to the countryside is complete without time around a campfire. So one night I used my camp skills to build a fire in the fire pit by the tire swing. As the darkness fell, we sat around roasting marshmallows, telling stories, enjoying each other's company. After getting our fill and feeling rather sticky, everyone retreated inside. My sister, Mary, and I lingered, looking up at the stars. I just love how when you look at stars at night, they just seem to multiply. The longer you look, the more you see. We stood there talking about the future, about the longing that comes when things are so nice and yet wishing to share it with a man. That seemed like the only missing piece. I try to be thankful, especially for my family, that we can get away together, and that we actually enjoy it. It seems like a rare thing these days, for people to like their families, and I know it. Is it selfish just to want a bit more? One more person to be mine forever to share the beautiful and the boring, the stars, the bluegrass, the cooking?

After the games and after the food and the entertainment, we'd go out to the screened-in porch. The silence of night was the perfect backdrop to unwind from our day of fun. The stars were out by the millions, putting on a glorious display for us. My sisters and I would cuddle up on the same day bed, holding still so the three of us would fit without being too uncomfortable or pushing the others off. We talked about life and mused about nothing with the ease that comes from spending a week with people you love. Just to be there, to be in close proximity, when normally we're so spread out was enough. We're not an overly physically affectionate family, but we wanted to be close, because we normally aren't. And there's something vulnerable about sharing that space. There's no bond like the sister bond.

On our last evening I slipped out before the games began to take a picture of the house at night, lit up from the inside. I like to think that if someone came upon that house that night, they'd watch the windows like a movie screen, knowing the family acting before them was full of love and life, happy, laughing and praying, silly and silent, content to be together in the Virginia countryside for one more night.

GETTING UNSTUCK

It's been a long summer. A long year really. Full of hard things and changes at my job – changes that I thought would make things better, which just ended up making things harder. I don't love change as it is, but when the change involves camp, which has not only been my job for almost nine years, but my life for that time and beyond, it creates huge ripples. Huge, stressful ripples. My camp family fell apart, almost all of us leaving our jobs at camp out of exhaustion, frustration, or frankly, because we'd been asked to. It's been heartbreaking, but somehow, at the same time, full of God's provision and direction.

Earlier this year I laid on my couch on a Saturday night, staring at the pictures framed on the wall in front of me, and I thought about how many nights I'd spent there on that couch watching TV, bored. So many friends had moved out of town, and I'd had a hard time meeting new friends in my same stage of life. I had joined a gym and a small group at church trying to spice up my life and be intentional about building community and getting out of the house, but I was still just feeling stuck, at an impasse in my own life. It didn't help that camp had been less satisfying as of late. I'd been doing that job for almost my whole adult life, and I don't

113

know if I was more efficient or less challenged, but either way it didn't bring the same fulfillment it had before, especially in the non-summer months. And so I'd spent too long just wanting things to be different. It became clear to me sitting there on my couch that something had to change. My life cannot look like this one year from now, I decided. It was a bold decision for me, and I had no idea what it would mean, but I decided to pray for a positive change in my life by October 1st, only about 7 months away. I wasn't necessarily praying for a new job, but I wanted to be open to that or anything else that would get me out of this rut.

It wasn't that I hadn't already been praying. For the past year or so, I'd been asking God almost daily what was next for me. Camp had been so so good, but the camp team had seen some turnover, and some of the vision for the future had gone with it. I couldn't have named it at the time, but that led the whole team to drift a little – drift through our days, getting things done, but not always being efficient or making strides towards new goals. I was still passionate about the summer, mostly the staff and the kids, but in general some of the magic had gone for me. I had essentially reached a dead end in my position, and I was ready for a challenge. It was becoming clear that this job, despite all the good, was not fulfilling in the same way it had once been.

The frustrations I'd easily overlooked before became key sticking points. The quirks of my coworkers that had been "just how they are" became major contentions. There were times I felt treated unfairly, and while I didn't always confront them aloud, when I did it was often met with platitudes or placation. I had to remind myself that I was working for God, not man, and until He led me elsewhere, camp was my assignment for better or for worse. But, I started asking myself more and more what it would look like for me to work somewhere else, and I even applied for a couple other jobs to no avail. That thought of leaving scared me, honestly. I was mostly comfortable where I was and only occasionally miserable. This was a really good job, I reminded myself. So many people would love to have a job like this. Camp jobs are not easy to come by, and at this one I was able to work in so many of my strengths. I had earned a lot of vacation time, I loved the people, and if I left I would miss the kids and the mountains and so much that had become so familiar and routine.

Plus, I really grew to love the people on my new team, and they truly made some of my most difficult days at camp a whole lot easier. They became family in a different way than previous teams, and I felt my role shift from peer to older sister, from someone with the same amount of experience to someone with several years more experience. I was one of the few who had been around the camp block a couple times, seen a lot of the camp scenarios and pitfalls, and was able to lend some insight and wisdom. I felt my legs become strong underneath me as I gave advice and made decisions. I was able to stand on my own without as many questions or second guesses. I became one of the only people at camp that people remembered from before. Parents knew to ask for me, business contacts knew they could trust me. I began to feel more and more confident in difficult situations; I was able to have hard conversations – confronting others in love or bringing up tough questions (of which there were many this year). I could stand my ground when I knew the answer should be no (or yes), and I knew where compromising our standards or making exceptions for staff or campers would lead since I'd seen it happen before. It had taken me almost nine years to get to this point, with my confidence in my abilities at an all-time high. How could I think of walking away now? I read something somewhere, no doubt on Pinterest or Facebook, that said, "It's not bad enough to leave, but not good enough to stay." That's exactly how I felt.

Even at the time I'd prayed my "Please, God, something by October 1st" prayer, change was stirring at camp, which was creating a lot of stress. Things were not looking good for the state of our team or the state of our summer. When my boss, who was a long-time friend and coworker, decided to step down and a new boss was hired right before the summer, the stress level was at a fever pitch. With the new boss came so many unknowns about the future of camp and the future of our team. It was the perfect storm from the get go with a lot of miscommunication, and several of us being pushed to our limit by the summer busyness compounded by trying to keep up with changes being made left and right. In our team's desperation, we prayed a lot, which was good and the only way we had any peace.

And I continued to try to keep a positive attitude – surely it wasn't as bad as it looked, surely things would turn around, surely this change of bosses would work out for our good, with a happy ending despite the difficult circumstances we found ourselves in. I had to continue to hope. Camp had been so near and dear to me and to all of the people on our staff team, and I couldn't just give up because of some unwelcome changes. We had put our literal blood, sweat and tears into the people and the place, but it felt like all that we knew, all we had worked for, was being stolen out of our hands, ripped right out from under us.

Camp was quickly becoming a place I didn't recognize, a place I didn't feel comfortable, a place where I felt pushed out of my very own home. Change was around every corner, popping up in the places I held sacred, in the traditions and routines that made camp what it was to me. The camp office, which had been my domain, a refuge in the busyness of summer, had been taken over by unfamiliar faces. Every interaction was a chance to practice showing grace and love – not an easy task in the throes of the summer.

Despite the changes and the difficulties of the transition, the summer was still full and rich with relationships and the stuff of camp that I loved. I savored each testimony told by kids on their last night, each story I heard from staff about lives being changed. I took every opportunity to get out of my office and meet with the staff girls I was mentoring. We went to coffee shops and for walks, took drives on the Blue Ridge Parkway and snuck away to get pedicures. I went with campers up to the Overlook as many times as I could. It had always been a favorite spot of mine because of the spectacular vantage point surrounded by layers upon layers of mountains while overlooking the valley below. I soaked up the rich staff worship rising from the dining hall before campers arrived each Saturday. I led our youngest staff through a book on camp counseling and planned girls' nights for the older staff. I would not let this summer pass me by because I was discouraged by the circumstances. I would live in every minute, even the hard minutes. I had to. I had to take it all in, because what if it was my last summer?

Midway through the summer, I called my mom when I was finally ready to think about the inevitable – it was probably time for me to leave camp. I sat just off the camp road at the picnic table near the BB gun range, a place with little foot traffic that time of morning, so I could speak freely. I didn't know how it would happen or when, but I knew my departure was coming, and I needed to process it. As we talked, I was incredulous, the anger and frustration rising. How could this place I loved so much be changing right in front of me? There was no way to stop the changes or the decisions that had been made by the new boss and the board above him, and it really didn't leave me much choice. This was no longer the camp I had known and loved, or it wouldn't be beyond this summer. Incredible sadness welled up inside of me, spilling out in tears I could not contain. Sure, I had been praying for months now for something new and for my next step to be abundantly clear, but I didn't want *this*. How could things end like this? It was wrong! It was unjust! And I wasn't ready to let it go.

I continued to pray, crying out to God for clarity, for strength to finish this season well, and for confirmation that He did in fact want me to leave my home and the comfort of camp. I knew it was probably God's will, but I just wanted to make extra sure. In July, I opened the devotional book I'd been using, Shauna Niequist's *Savor*, and the title of that day's devotion was "Leaving My Job." My heart beat faster as I looked at the title from the day before, which I'd skipped over – "Nothing to Lose" – something I'd said to myself over and over this year as I'd pushed back on unwise decisions and had hard conversations. God was making it abundantly clear, leaving no room for doubt.

It was obvious now. God was showing me my time at camp was about to end, but I still wasn't sure how to pull the plug. Later that week, I went into a conversation with the new boss wanting to explain a few things and give him some perspective on why I thought this transition had been a hard one for all of us. And in that conversation I felt I was being asked to leave. The new boss did the hard work of picking a time for me. On the one hand, I couldn't believe what I had heard. On the other hand, God had been preparing me for this moment for months. I would leave my job at the end of the summer.

After that conversation, I walked through the rest of the day in a fog. I didn't know what to do next or how to compute what I'd heard. I didn't know who to tell and what to tell them. Should I call my mom sobbing or carry on with my day as normal? I was in shock, feeling every emotion from confusion to fear to sadness, yet with the slightest bit of relief mixed in.

My life, as I knew it, was going to drastically change at the end of the summer, but there were still three weeks of summer sessions left. I determined to keep my head held high for those remaining few weeks. I would rise above any drama, keep my integrity intact, go above and beyond, despite any awkward interactions and every presumptuous confrontation. I would not give anyone anything bad to say about me in this transition, and I would do my best to keep the gossip mill from flowing. I had poured out my life at camp, and that is what I wanted to be remembered of me.

I also decided to feel all the feelings that I knew would come – I didn't want to stuff anything down only to have it bubble back up at a later time. I wanted to feel the weight of the sadness, the anger, the injustice and the incredible gratitude. I renewed my desire to savor it all, and I wanted every minute to count. I wanted to have the most fun, the most laughs, the most spiritually impacting everything! That did put some pressure on some things, but it also made me want to linger – sit around the dinner table a little longer, stay up a little later, play a little harder. I wanted to go out with a bang, doing all the fun things I loved about camp – dance to "Cotton Eyed Joe" on the last night, go on outings for milkshakes or Waffle House, go night swimming, laugh hard playing Chubby Bunny, and not spend too much time holed up in my office. Those last three weeks would be the best I could make them—for myself and for the people around me.

On the last night of camp, the campers have an opportunity to get up and share what God has done in their lives that week. We sit at the outdoor amphitheater with a campfire, even though it's often too hot to sit close. We listen to the cicadas, loud and proud, doing their best to drown out the low murmur of antsy campers sitting on uncomfortable benches. Sometimes fireflies light up the night, putting on a show. I look up to the canopy of trees overhead and think about all the times I've sat in that place, worshipping, listening to how God has worked. On this last night of camp, the very last of the summer, I was facilitating the sharing. It was our biggest week of camp on record, a throw-back to glory days of full camp weeks when I had been a counselor. I stood on the stage at the end of the evening, as we closed by singing "Jesus Loves Me" like we'd done a thousand times before, and my heart was so full. That had been my mantra, my creed, for almost every talk I'd given – Jesus loves you, Jesus loves you. If there was anything I wanted people to walk away with from camp, anything I'd want them to remember one year, five years, ten years from now that was it -- Jesus loved them.

I watched as the campers and staff, silhouetted by the campfire and the path lights, wrapped their arms around each other and sang. I couldn't make out any faces through the darkness, through the light of the campfire, but I could see the outlines of the crowd. It could have been 10 years before, it looked and sounded the same. I love those timeless traditions of camp. I loved that God allowed me to the be one standing in the front on that last night of the summer, leading the song, watching the kids, listening to the sounds ring out for one last time. God was good to allow closure in that way, and I knew it was His gift to me.

As hard as it was for me to prepare for the end of this era, it was compounded by the fact that I wasn't the only one leaving camp. Four of the five people who had been on the team when the new boss was hired were also leaving at the end of the summer. Word got out among the summer staff, despite my desire to keep it hush hush in an effort not to distract from the remaining few weeks of camp, but no one made a formal announcement until the morning after our last campers left. It was a staff fun day – we were taking them whitewater rafting before our end of summer celebration banquet that night.

The five full-time team members gathered behind the dining hall to discuss who would say what. We circled up to pray, standing close, holding hands, touching shoulders, needing each other's strength. The year we had been through together was a doozey. We'd spent many hours in prayer together, pleading with God for His help and his direction. We'd called each other to higher standards, needing the others desperately to rise up, to be there to pull off the many jobs of summer camp. We had been a team in the truest sense of the word, and the five of us were survivors – bonded from an experience no one else could share with us. As we prayed, my tears slipped out unexpectedly, despite trying to keep them in just a little longer. I was going to miss this team, this place, and the moments when we'd all been in it together.

We gathered all the summer staff on the front porch, everyone in their bathing suits and shorts, wrapped in towels, ready to go rafting. Of course we'd make the biggest announcement of the summer marking one of the most significant changes in my life in our bathing suits. It felt fitting to be completely informal and vulnerable in that way. I looked around at all the familiar faces, my friends, the staff I'd grown to love, and with my fellow full-time team by my side, I told them I'd be leaving. Leaving camp and our family. And then my three friends said the same. I saw faces around the circle redden, with tears welling up, slipping down, no one even trying to stop them. I looked at all the staff, the stories they represented in my life, and I felt the weight of the moment, savoring it too. So much of my life had happened there on that porch and in the cabins up the hill, and although this was one of the hardest moments, I still wanted to remember every part of it.

In the days and months that followed my departure from camp, I felt everything all over again, reliving every good and painful moment from the summer. Oh man, there was so much pain – so many feelings of anger, disbelief and loss. And just when I thought I was moving on, a memory would bring it all back to the surface again. Despite all the hard parts, I kept coming back around to God's goodness and his faithfulness. Sara Groves' rendition of "Great is Thy Faithfulness" played in my car most of the summer so that every time I'd get in I'd remember – "all I have needed, his hand will provide…" In this season especially, I didn't feel abandoned by God in the slightest. I knew He was there, in it with me and us. He cared deeply for me and put others in this summer to show me that too. I needed that. I needed Him to be close. I needed Him to carry me through the really long days and nights, through the really awkward meetings and the painful goodbyes, through the emotions heightened by the changes happening...and through the forgiveness too – which I'm still working on. He met me on the mountaintops (literally, at times), and in the deepest of lows, when I cried and needed his strength to carry me through the next day, hour, and minute. He did it. All that I'd asked, including my prayer to make my next step abundantly clear, was answered. There was no doubt in my mind that my time at camp was up, and even in the negative feelings that came with that, there was an underlying sense of freedom. I felt gloriously unstuck. The change I wanted so badly on my couch that spring came about in the most unexpected and unwelcome way, but He was faithful to me through it.

And it wasn't even October 1st yet.

HOME

It's interesting how a house becomes a home. There's no recipe or formula, but somehow, over time, the place where you live, where you sleep at night, where you've been sick and well, happy and sad, becomes a witness to your life. It's a shelter in literal and figurative storms, a place to gather friends, to hang pictures, to cook meals and laugh until you cry. I have loved my little apartment –my home– in Asheville for the past eight and a half years. It has become a part of me, an integral part of my well-being over this time, and now, as I prepare to move out and move on, I'm not ready to leave it behind.

The apartment was a gift from the very beginning. Such a good gift. I'd decided I'd try living alone for a season and sought the perfect place for my new venture. Not wanting to live in an apartment complex, I looked for an apartment attached to a house, preferably with a Christian family as my landlords. I prayed for a yard and oh, a fire pit would be a nice addition too. It needed to be close to camp, and I had my eye on one area in particular.

When I saw an ad for an apartment in the location I wanted, I called right away. I was a little gun shy after seeing a couple small places I knew I could never live in. They'd been dingy and unappealing, and please, God, don't let those be my only options. God and my mom had reminded me that even though those weren't good options, it didn't mean there would not be a perfect place for me. I just hadn't seen it yet. Until this place. It was an apartment on the ground floor of a house set into the hillside. The front door faced the backyard, but the potential landlords let me in through the garage. When I entered the apartment into the kitchen, angels may as well have been singing in the background, and a huge smile spread across my face. There was light streaming in the window, the ceilings were high, despite being in the basement, and the cabinets were tall. The living room to my right had more big windows! The bedroom was huge with a long walk-in closet and built in shelves. There was a yard, a parking space in the three-car garage, lots of storage and lots of potential. Where do I sign?

Before my mom brought my stuff from my storage unit at home, I spent my first night in my new place on the floor, too excited to stay with friends any longer. I went to a concert with friends that night and when I got back, I realized I was missing an earring, which seems so trivial, but it was an important earring. I bought those earrings on a trip I took to Chile while I was living in Wisconsin. We had been on a mission trip to help at another camp and did some backpacking, and that trip had been such a bright spot in an otherwise pretty difficult year. Those earrings represented that trip to me. While I was out, one earring had gotten caught on my scarf and fell out, nowhere to be seen again. I cried on my new apartment floor about those earrings. This was home now, a safe place for me to feel the depth of emotion that comes within the comfort of your own four walls, even if it's over the silliest of losses.

It wasn't until I had been living in the new apartment for a little while that I realized it was everything I'd asked for.

The family upstairs was a Christian family. I was close to camp in the specific area I had wanted to live. There was a big yard and a fire pit sat at the back of the lot. The fire pit had really been an afterthought in my prayers, something I threw out to God as an aside. It would be fun, but certainly not necessary. Although I didn't end up using the fire pit that much (something about working at a camp and already smelling like campfire a lot through the prime fire pit seasons), it wasn't really about the usefulness of it, rather the way it caused me to remember. It represented an answered prayer, a wish on a whim. It represented God's goodness to me and the way He not only knows what I need, but what I want too. And He cares about those things just as much.

Sitting on an air mattress for a couch got old quickly, so I bought my first pieces of adult furniture (my couch's name was The Comfy and boy, what a good first purchase) and an adult-sized TV that was bigger than the throw pillow sized one I had in college. I hung pictures and bought dishes and lit candles, settling in. I went for walks in the neighborhood, hoping to find better cell phone reception, and made plans to have friends over and family visit. As the weather got warmer, I opened windows, letting the spring air breathe life into each crevice. I left them open long after the night air got cold, cuddling under blankets, breathing deeply. The smell of fresh air in the apartment was one that brought back memories every time – of being newly moved in, excited about what spring would hold. Living alone meant I could let the cold air in and also decorate as I wanted, clean when I wanted, and do whatever I wanted in my new home.

It did get lonely at times, living by myself. I missed having someone ask me about my day when I got home or share in cooking dinner and cleaning up afterwards. And it could be boring – with no roommates just to hang out in the doldrums of the day. And occasionally it was scary. There were lots of bumps in the night, many I got used to, but always new ones that would strike fear in my heart of the lurkers outside waiting to break in or just being creepy. (I quickly learned not to watch anything remotely scary or intense on TV, as that did not do good things for my imagination.) But every time I thought about moving out, going somewhere with a roommate, all the good things about living alone in that place would come rushing to the front of my mind – the way the afternoon sun shone in the living room windows, the two trees in the backyard that my hammock hung perfectly between, and the way the bedroom stayed cool and dark in the mornings, ideal for sleeping in.

When I felt really alone, there was great comfort in The Family Upstairs, as I called them to most friends, looking out for me. There was a night I was wishing for a roommate as I headed out to run errands. Driving away, I told God aloud, "I just wish I had someone to leave the light on for me." As I was out and about, my landlord called to see if I was coming home that night. He said, "I just wanted to see if I should leave the light on for you." The Family Upstairs came through for me in more ways than they ever knew. The daughters brought me homemade treats. The dog, Molly, stopped barking at me eventually and kept me company out in the yard. Just knowing they were upstairs provided me a level of comfort and security that I needed at times when I freaked myself out. They called to check on me if they hadn't seen me or my car for a couple days. They invited me up for drinks with the neighbors and made room in the driveway for my friends to park. They were kind and gracious and another good gift. My only complaint was the smell of cooking bacon that would waft down on Saturday mornings, waking me up and taunting me. But, honestly, they probably would have offered me some if I had asked.

Despite The Family Upstairs, I would still worry about being alone, especially when I got sick. Sometimes I would morbidly think about the fact that I could die in the night and no one would know for quite some time. There was a time when I had a mysterious stomach issue, and I was in so much pain I didn't know what to do. I went to the doctor, which I hardly ever do, and he ruled out all the obvious things. He gave me something for the pain and I went home to try to sleep it off. I prayed a lot while I was awake for God's healing, for His mercy, and for Him to take that pain away. In my delirious, sick state, I slept fitfully, but when I would roll over and wake up slightly, I was aware of someone else in the room, watching over me, helping me with my covers. When I actually woke up enough to be fully aware of my surroundings, I was so surprised that I was alone. I like to think that an angel stood guard that night (as I think they do every night), but made his presence known, so I would know I was not alone.

My apartment has been a safe place for me, a refuge when life felt hard, a place where God met me and where I felt his frustrating silence. It allowed me to cry, to wallow, to pray out loud, fervent or timid. It was a soft place for my heart to land when it had been bruised or bumped or broken. I found myself wanting to be there, knowing everything felt better at home. I shed many tears there, laughed heartily there, and shared secrets and dreams there. It seems strange to find so much comfort in the confines of these walls, to find security in a building, in a home, but this apartment has become like a friend in and of itself. And so I found myself mourning the loss of it before I even left.

I didn't host a lot of big parties at the apartment. I preferred to have a few people over at a time, but after this past summer, my last at camp, I threw a party for several friends as a celebration of the summer two nights after the summer sessions were over. I was exhausted. The summer had not afforded me the luxury of sleeping my full nine hours a night, and I certainly hadn't caught back up in those two nights. The apartment was still in complete disarray, since I hadn't had time to unpack from living out at camp, and I was feeling the mixed emotions that came from the end of the summer and the end of an era.

I thought of Shauna Niequist's book *Bread and Wine* and the healing powers of gathering around the table for a meal. I didn't feel up for it. I bought rotisserie chickens and some brownies from the grocery store, and asked friends to bring sides and extras I had forgotten, so I didn't have to put forth very much effort. I threw all my bags and boxes from camp into the bedroom and shut the door, put on a dress and a little makeup, and waited for the doorbell to ring. Several friends had never been to my apartment before, so I was pleased to have them over for one last celebration. We built a fire in the fire pit and had a few drinks. We laughed and some cried, and we celebrated what had been and what we had been through together. We stayed up way later than we should have on a work night, and hung on to the last few hours of us all being together under one roof. I was glad it was my roof, my fire pit, my home to share with some of my closest friends.

My mom has often told me the story of when she was preparing to move out of a house she loved. It was when my parents were first married and my sister was a baby. She loved the house they lived in and she wasn't sure she would ever get to live in a place quite so cute, quite so perfect for her again. She tells of how she was standing out in the yard, and God told her that she should appreciate that house while she had it, to enjoy every last piece, and then when she moved, she wouldn't miss it so much. She would know that she had gotten all it had to offer her during the season their paths crossed. I think of that story often, and I try to practice that too. I tried that at my home, especially as I prepared to move out, to love every minute, even the lonely minutes, to breathe in the fresh air, wallow in the green grass of the yard, be thankful for the noise of The Family Upstairs, and allow God to meet me here yet again.

I slept on the floor again my last night there. My stuff is all moved out now, and my car is packed. I laid awake for a while, despite being exhausted, knowing it had come full circle, thankful for the good gift of this house that had become home, and hoping to find another home again very soon.

CROSS COUNTRY

"So, what's next?"

It was the inevitable question. My job at camp had just ended in a somewhat dramatic fashion and everyone wanted to know what my plan was.

"I'm going to take some time off and travel. Drive across the country, actually. I'm going to stay with my sister and her family in California for a while."

Their faces would light up, "You are?" they'd say enthusiastically. "That's great! Who is going with you?"

"I'm going by myself," I'd say confidently, trying to convince myself it would be fine.

And then I'd usually get a wary, "Oh, really?" or a cautionary, "Are you sure that's a good idea?"

I'd smile and nod, and then tell myself defensively, "It's just driving. It's not like I'm hitchhiking across the country." Going solo wasn't ideal, I'll admit, but most people I knew had jobs and lives and couldn't just pick up and leave for a road trip with little notice. Heck, I didn't actually want to be leaving either. I loved my home in Asheville. I hesitantly packed up my apartment, taking it in small doses, delaying the inevitable. On the other hand, it excited me more than it worried me to finally have the chance to drive across the country, which had been a bucket list item since college. After much prayer, I decided I'd be fine going it alone, much to my dad's chagrin.

I understood the mixed bag of envy and excitement, bewilderment and caution, because I had a mixture of emotions swirling too. Traveling across the country is a grand adventure, one I had wanted to take at some point in my life. But I didn't really want to go by myself, or necessarily even go at all, at least not now, not under these circumstances. It felt like I was being pushed out of my life, having to leave my job and my landlords putting their house, and therefore my apartment, on the market, which meant I had to move. I wanted adventure when I wanted adventure, not when it was thrust upon me. And even though I had been ready for a change, praying for it desperately, actually, I had grown quite comfortable with where I was. The circumstances surrounding my upcoming move felt totally unfair and totally not how I imagined. And yet, I also knew it was right. The time was now. I knew it was time to go, and with my sister and her family willing to let me crash for a couple months, I packed my bags and headed west.

I hit the road on October 1st, a cloudy, cool day that felt fitting for my mood. It was dreary and a little portending, like the clouds just wanted to break and let out all they were holding in.

I stopped downtown to eat breakfast, maybe write a little, but I just didn't have it in me. I didn't want to write, because I didn't want to feel all the emotions lurking right under the surface. I just wanted to get on the road and get leaving over with. As I pulled out of town, I took a long look at the back of camp's mountain. "Goodbye, camp. Goodbye, Asheville," I said aloud. The tears started welling up in my eyes, but I held them in. I wasn't ready to start mourning yet, and I wasn't sure what would happen when I did. The weight of impending change was getting too heavy to carry, but I continued to drag it along behind me, until it was absolutely necessary to let it go.

My first stop was Murray, Kentucky, a town I lived in for six years from ages three to nine. The irony of starting a new chapter by going back to an old one was not lost on me. As I pulled into town, I realized I was about to go right by my old elementary school. Even though it was 4:30 in the afternoon on a weekday, the parking lot was empty and no lights were on. I got out of the car, looking around to see if there was someone I should ask about being there. Not seeing anyone, I walked around and took it all in as the memories came pouring into my mind. I stood in this parking lot 27 years ago, crying with my mom, not sure I could actually go into my kindergarten classroom. I had lined up on that wall, waiting to be picked up after school, avoiding the boy who teased me. I peeked in a couple windows and walked down to the playground, remembering the friends and the laughter and some of the injuries too. I remembered the cold plastic of the tire swing and the rusty pole it hung on that had given me a black eye when my brother "accidently" pushed me into it. I walked beyond the playground and breathed deeply. I used to love the way it smelled out here – fresh and woodsy and like grass. In the woods on the other side of the field, there had been a bridge over a creek and sometimes our teachers took us out there to explore. I smiled at the memories, and texted my mom and brother a couple pictures. "It looks exactly the same," my brother replied, even though in person the age was more apparent. It felt smaller, sadder. It didn't do justice to the childhood memories I had there.

I had made plans to stay the night with my sister Erin's best friend who I've only spent small amounts of time with as an adult, the last time being at Erin's wedding eight years ago. She welcomed me into her art studio and her apartment in the back. We chatted as peers, and as we stood up to go to dinner, she asked, "Have you always been that tall?" "Not always," I said, "but since I've stopped growing, yes." Maybe something about being back in the town where she knew me as a child made it seem like I should be shorter. When she paid for my dinner, I was reminded how many people I had in my corner, rooting for me, excited for me, willing to help me during this transition.

After dinner, she drove me around town and memories came flooding back. Where was the giant boot that used to sit on the roof of that shoe store? The eight year old in me was really disappointed it was gone. We drove by the high school where she and my sisters had attended – where Mary had taken me to their Mardi Gras festival, and where I won a cake at the cakewalk. We turned left, and left again to go by my old house. I smiled, recounting in my mind the thousands of memories in that yard, in that house, in that neighborhood – riding my bike down that street wishing desperately I was a twin, playing kickball with the neighborhood boys, climbing the tree in the front yard. They were all good memories, reminding me that I had a happy and carefree childhood.

The next morning I said goodbye to my friend and made my way towards St. Louis. I had never been to the Arch, the Gateway to the West, and it felt fitting to go now. I needed to go as part of the driving cross country experience. I took the small tram to the top, crammed in with two other adults, feeling conspicuous being by myself. I took a few pictures and that was that, but I felt like it should have been more. I should explore or walk around downtown or spend more time up at the top. But with no one to experience it with, I felt I had accomplished my mission and westward I went.

After St. Louis, the enormity of the country started to set in. I wasn't even to the middle of the country yet, and I still had a long way to go, lots of road ahead. I had already been enjoying my "funemployment" for six weeks before I left town, so I had grown accustomed to not doing much with my days. I just carried that over into my road trip. I decided to settle in, enjoy the journey, and I would get there when I got there.

It's good I set my mind on enjoying the journey early on, because although the United States is a vast and varied country, Kansas is not so varied, just vast. It was all that everyone said it would be – long and flat and wide open. I spent the night with some friends outside of Kansas City, and spent much of the next day plodding through Kansas. It was exactly as I pictured it, even though part of me hadn't believed it actually existed as they said it did. There was so much open space, fields farther than the eye could see. I couldn't even tell where the land met the sky since the clouds and the fall landscape didn't provide much variation. I had to laugh to myself though. "I can't believe I'm doing this. I'm driving across the country – through Kansas – by myself." After feeling stuck in my job and in my life for so long, it was good for my soul to be out in the expanse of cornfields, miles and miles of cornfields. I was a little surprised by the beauty, even in all its desolate existence. And just as the low, dark clouds fit my mood leaving Asheville, somehow Kansas fit too. It fit what was to come–endless opportunities and room to breathe.

After Kansas, my eyes were ready for a bit of scenery change. "Welcome to Colorful Colorado." The sign greeted me as I passed the state line. I wanted mountains and lots of them, but eastern Colorado was flatter than I was expecting. It was still beautiful and colorful with big sky covered in wispy, hazy clouds that cast shadows over the open horizon. The whole landscape had a bit of a blue, ethereal feel – more wide-open space, more room for me to breathe, to remember, to be thankful. The road rose and fell with views of the plateaus ever changing.

I had a lot of time to think on this trip. I had a lot of time to do a lot actually – listen to music and podcasts and call friends when I had reception. Being silent for a while became a priority too. It's not often that I have hours and hours to be still, to pray, to listen. Almost every day on the road as I thanked God for this opportunity, for the beautiful countryside, I would get a little teary. I was so overcome with how good God had been to me, how he provided the time and the resources to take this trip, how he knew it was what my heart needed. It had been a dream to drive across the country for so long – and I was doing it! God has been so kind to fulfill this dream, even under these circumstances, and I didn't want to take that for granted. There was never a time I felt bored– antsy maybe, tired of being in the car definitely– but never bored. And on that day especially, the anticipation of those great Rocky Mountains kept me engaged in the last few hours of my drive.

Denver is apparently in the shadow of the Rockies, but clouds blocked my view both days I was there. An old camp friend opened her home to me and acted as my tour guide. We got out into the Rockies one day, behind the clouds – stopping at turn offs to take pictures of magnificent views of lakes and mountains behind. We went out among the bright yellow aspens, taking more pictures with self-timers and laughing long and hard at how ridiculous we felt taking picture after picture hoping for our next Instagram-worthy shot. We hiked up to St. Mary's Glacier – only a three quarter mile hike - but difficult for me in the high altitude. It started to sprinkle as we got to the glacier, so we cut our time short, but not before I took in every angle – the blue water, the tall pines, the silence. We spent the rest of our time eating good food and watching bad movies, and giggling about boys and stories we hadn't told each other before. We talked about old friends and new friends and new possibilities. She took me downtown one evening, and we camped out in Union Station planning to partake in happy hour, but eating Twix ice cream instead. Denver was the perfect pit stop – perfect to be with an old friend who made me laugh, but could understand the heartache that came with the disappointment of camp ending. We met in the in between, the uncomfortable middle – where true friends can connect without pretense, without expectation – with ease and laughter and ice cream.

I left Denver with my sights set on Salt Lake City, and after a quick detour through Arches National Park (worth it!), I was on my way. Because I'm a cautious/paranoid traveler, I had tried to avoid driving at night, especially in unfamiliar territory, but that wasn't going to happen that day. It was mid-afternoon by the time I left Arches, and I still had several hours to go. I tried to enjoy the sunset on my left reflecting off the mountains on my right as I drove north through Utah, even though the vast landscape with miles and miles of no civilization put a little knot in my stomach. I talked to a friend on the phone for a while, until the mountains cut off my reception. Then I watched the bars on my phone go from zero to one to two to four and back again over and over while I drove through the pitch-black mountain passes. I wanted to enjoy the stars, the scarcity of civilization, but I also just wanted to get to the city. Nervousness attempted to overtake my joy that dark night. I felt very alone out there, vulnerable without the option to phone a friend if needed. "I'm just driving. Nothing is going to happen. God is with me," I spoke and prayed into the night. It was a conscious choice to push away the feelings of paranoia, to trust God's unseen hand. Passing by plumes of white smoke coming from a plant distracted me for a few minutes, and then before I knew it, I rounded a bend to see the lights of Provo in the distance. I sighed with relief, a little embarrassed to have been so concerned.

Later, I realized my trip through Utah's mountain passes that night was the story of the last year of my life played out in four hours. It started off sunny and bright, and having just completed an adventure in Arches, I was on a high, but I knew by the setting sun that darkness was to follow. All through the pitch black twists and turns of the last year, I had wanted to call someone to wave a wand to take away the uncomfortable nature of the unknown or at least distract me from it. I said I trusted God, and I said I wanted to go where He led, but I actually wanted a sure thing with bright lights and cell phone reception to guide my path. And even though logically I was quite safe inside my reliable car with my GPS – as I was in God's hands through the ever-changing circumstances and upheaval of the last year – the what ifs lingered out there getting louder and louder until I quelled my doubts and fears with prayer, faith and common sense. Once the city lights came into view and my destination was in reach, even though it was still unfamiliar territory, I could breathe easier. There was a city on the other side. I was heading in the right direction. And there was hope for a new day once I got there. Whew. What a ride.

When I was planning this part of my trip, I found out my dad would be in Salt Lake City on business the same time I planned to be there. I would say coincidentally, except that I had prayed a lot about where I would stay specifically in Salt Lake City. Conveniently, I was able to stay with my dad in Snowbird, right outside the city. When I met some of my dad's work colleagues the next day, they of course asked me about my job situation. "Well, I'm in between jobs right now. Just driving across the country and staying with my sister for a couple months." I tried to sound confident, like this was totally normal and fine with me, but I squirmed a little as I realized for the first time how uncomfortable it is not to have a job or a home or a place to go back to. In my hours of driving, I had grown to like the idea that I was living life to the fullest, taking advantage of this unexpected time off, but when I had to explain it to older business men, it fell a little flat, felt irresponsible even. They looked concerned, cocking their heads to the side as if wondering if they'd heard me correctly. My dad tried to interject, "Well, you have some prospects when you go back," which was true, I suppose, but felt so out of reach in that moment. Those prospects still had months to materialize. I'd only been on the road six days. And I hadn't really thought about it before then, how Asheville wasn't really my home anymore. My stuff was still there, but in storage. I didn't have a camp job – or any job – as a security blanket or as a place to put my identity. I was just "in between" – in between jobs, in between cities, in between everything. I wanted to shout, "I'm enjoying myself, okay? This has been fun and cathartic and just what I wanted!" Instead, I smiled politely. "Nice to meet you."

After a day in Salt Lake and an overnight pit stop in Reno (Nevada is another rather empty state – even the towns on the map were blink-and-you'll-miss-them spots), I was only a few hours away from my sister's house in the Bay Area. Coming into the home stretch, I drove across a giant bridge and I felt like I was floating – into the grand expanse of the blue sky, the blue water, the euphoria of having driven almost 3000 miles across 10 states in the past 9 days by myself with a little help from my friends along the way.

I pulled into town and into my sister's driveway with a little disbelief still hanging on. This trip had been largely about the journey, and now with the destination under my feet, the unsettled feeling lingered. But maybe that was good for me – good for me to be in the in between a bit longer, good for me to take my life and this transition one day at a time. Just enjoy life on the west coast with my sister, a safe place after a hard season and a once in a lifetime trip.

EPILOGUE:
WHEN THE ROAD FEELS LONG

I hiked up the hill behind my sister's house in California, which had been a favorite spot in previous visits. Her house sits on a peninsula and from that vantage point you can see the water on all three sides and the Golden Gate Bridge in the distance. I sat down at the top, away from family, away from my phone and Facebook, and all the ways I'd tried to distract myself, and I cried. They were tears I didn't know I needed to shed, because surely I was finished feeling sad by now. But I mourned the life I had left behind. I mourned the friendships that would change and the life I thought I would lead. I cried because I loved my little Asheville apartment, and I missed the Blue Ridge Mountains and my friends.

It's been two years now since I left for California, and almost that long since I've been back east in my new job at another camp. And some days I question if this was the right move at all – if I missed something by taking this job, if this is really what God wanted. It's been hard to start again somewhere new, and especially in my first year here, my heart hurt to think about all I left behind. There was no doubt in my mind that it was time to move on from my other job, but I didn't think the transition would be so difficult. I thought about all the ways I thought my life would turn out, about how I thought I'd have gotten married in Asheville because it was such a pretty place, how my friends there would hold my babies, and how, even after I'd left my job at camp there, I'd always be able to go back and it would still be home. There have been times in these past two years when I have closed my eyes, breathed deeply, and somehow transported myself back to the mountains and back to the life I had known so well. Then when I opened my eyes and saw my current, unfamiliar surroundings I felt what could only be described as dismay.

It's true isn't it - that life doesn't always turn out like you hope or expect? That the road I thought I was on towards my life goals and fulfillment has a thousand more twists and turns than I wanted or welcomed. And yet, I still plod along taking the good with the bad, the scenic vistas with the muddy ditches, remembering God's faithfulness doesn't run out because of my doubt.

When I allow myself to stay in a place of longing and disappointment, my heart feels heavy. My circumstances are too much to bear alone, and the road feels long with many more potholes than mountaintops. There have been days, in these two years and several times before that, when I've just wanted to give up. I've wanted to say no thank you to any more challenges, any more disappointment or any more "that's not how I thought this was going to look." I wanted things to turn out how I wanted them to turn out with that guy, with that job, with that friend, and dang it, this life shouldn't always be this hard. I've cried out to God again and again to show me where He's leading and sometimes I've just cried – hot, salty tears, angry that God isn't who I thought He was, acting in the ways I thought He would.

Why didn't He always give me exactly what I wanted, what I knew to be His best?

But, then I'm reminded to keep my eyes up and fixed on God. I give him thanks. I put on some worship music and sing loudly to drown out the negative feelings. I call a friend to get some perspective, because nothing sinks me faster than staying in my own head for too long. I realize again that to say no thank you to the unknowns and challenges of life (as if I have that choice) and to give up when the going gets tough, is to say no to hope. Because I can't tune out the hard parts of life without turning off the part of my heart that hopes the best is yet to come and that maybe this time will be different. In shutting off any part of my heart, I may also unintentionally tune out the part that remembers who God says He is and takes Him at His word, and I need that to propel me forward when I just want to stop. These feelings and decisions are all connected in my heart and in my mind, and to stay soft to life, despite its challenges, is to stay soft to God.

I want to stay soft to God. Oh man, do I. In my heart of hearts, when I look past my insecurities and my doubts, and just listen to Him, when I settle my heart and my mind long to enough to really hear Him, I hear it again and again – "I love you, daughter. I'm for you. I'm not holding out on you." I struggle against it – a lot actually – more than I want to admit, because I continue to believe the lie that He is not enough, that if He really loved me He'd come through for me in the ways I've wanted him to. And yet, He continues to pursue me, to remind me of truth. He showed me again recently that contentment is a choice. And while this new job and town may not be exactly what I wanted for myself, I can choose to be content because I trust that He brought me here, and He did in fact graciously provide this very life I'm now leading. Or I can writhe and wrestle and just generally be miserable.

God has brought that old worship song, "The More I Seek You," back to mind recently – "I wanna...lay back against you and breathe, feel your heart beat." He's reminded me of Jesus' disciple John reclining on Him at the table at the Last Supper – fully present with Jesus, fully relaxed. That is where I want to be. I want to recline against Him, completely trusting His heart toward me, his motives with my circumstances and the unknown of what's to come. It is a choice. It is a choice I have to make multiple times a day sometimes. And so I'm re-learning and remembering to trust.

When I think back over these stories I've told here and over the other stories of my life, there have certainly been days when feelings of sadness and disappointment have clouded my vision. Despair lurked around dark corners trying to take me out and leave me on the road, my limping slowing to a stop. But then I see a glimpse of God's goodness in friendship, in mountains, in His word, in unexpected laughter, and I allow hope to poke rays of sunshine into the gloom. I put one foot in front of the other, and I continue to follow God down the road, his faithfulness quietly guiding me until I'm ready to fully trust Him again, until I'm ready to run after Him with all I have. He's been there all along, you know – through all the days of all these pages and beyond – and as long as I'm still walking the road of life, I want to stay close to Him, hold his hand as he leads me around more and more turns. Each time I say yes to him, despite unanswered questions, the easier it becomes to remember his great faithfulness the next time I feel weary. And if nothing else in my future works out like I thought it would, may I continue to live out this glorious adventure with God through all the days of my life.

ACKNOWLEDGMENTS

I would like to thank the many people who helped me get these words out of my head and in to a real-life book. Thanks to those of you who believed I could do it, who thought I had something valuable to say, and promised to read it, too.

Thank you to the readers of early chapters, namely Erin and Jen, who read *rough* drafts, saw the potential, and encouraged me to keep going. I'm very grateful to Lacey who copyedited, Ashton and Lana for reading a close-to-finished draft, and Mom and Mary who only gave positive feedback. Thanks to Eden for your honesty and editing skills. And to Tiffany, your great cover art is all I wanted it to be!

And a big thank you to all my friends who asked, "How is the book coming?" That question alone propelled me to the finish line.

Finally, thank you to those of you who let me tell, in these pages, the parts of your stories that intersected with mine. My life is richer with you in it!

ABOUT THE AUTHOR

Abby Friend is a thirtysomething writer and adventurer who has spent her adult life working at summer camp. She loves getting outside, traveling to new places, exploring the mountains, playing trivia games, and relaxing in her hammock. You can reach her at abby.friend15@gmail.com.

Made in the USA
Monee, IL
10 May 2020